DESTINED FOR THE TOP

Books by Dr. Joe Ibojie

*Bible-Based Dictionary of Prophetic Symbols
for Every Christian*—New

The Watchman—New

Dreams and Visions Volume 1—International Best Seller

Dreams and Visions Volume 2—New

The Justice of God: Victory in Everyday Living—New

How to Live the Supernatural Life in the Here and Now—
International Best Seller

Illustrated Bible-Based Dictionary of Dream Symbols—
International Best Seller

Dreams and Visions Volume 1—Korean translation

Dreams and Visions Volume 1—Italian translation

Illustrated Bible-Based Dictionary of Dream Symbols—
Korean translation

Destined for the Top—New

Available from Cross House Books

DR. JOE IBOJIE

DESTINED FOR THE TOP

Overcoming Life Issues That May Hold You Down!

Includes Exclusive Happy Married Life Manual

CROSS HOUSE BOOKS
Christian Book Publishers
245 Midstocket Road
Aberdeen
AB15 5PH, UK

"The entrance of Your Word brings light."

ISBN: 978-0-9564008-5-7

For Worldwide Distribution, Printed in U.S.A.

1 2 3 4 5 6 / 14 13 12 11

To order products by Dr. Joe Ibojie & other Cross House Books,

contact sales@crosshousebooks.co.uk.

Other correspondence: info@crosshousebooks.co.uk.

Visit www.crosshousebooks.co.uk.

Dedication

I dedicate this book to Bishop and Bishop (Mrs.) Addo, my mentors. Through them, my wife and I have learned the true meaning of the supernatural love of God put into practice. They are beacons of the light of God to many people; and through their unswerving commitment to our welfare, I have learned that I, too, can love God with all I have—body, soul, and spirit.

In my early Christian years, they believed in me even when I did not have the faith myself. I miss the times I spent with them in my formative years in Christian living—those were the times I received the teachings that nurtured me and are the fundamentals that still propel me to this day! All I can say is, to God be the glory for great things He has done!

Endorsements

We are so thankful for our dear friend and brother, Dr. Joe Ibojie. The skill and wisdom he writes with grows with each publication. This latest book, *Destined for the Top,* is a veritable goldmine with each chapter containing nuggets of truth and wisdom for developing a strong biblical foundation in our lives based on application of scriptural truth. It is an excellent resource for both the new and more mature believer, providing a comprehensive tool for personal discipleship and mentoring others.

Yvonne Ewen, Leader
Riverside Movement, Riverside Church Network
Banff, Scotland

Destined for the Top is for everyone and another classic from Dr. Joe Ibojie. This book teaches on the mundane things of our daily living as they reflect on how to handle the issues that life may throw at us. You will learn how to turn your trials and failures into opportunities to move forward with a life of purpose. It offers wisdom and deep insight on how to make the best of your marriage and realize that the essence at all times is getting closer to God and with your mate.

No matter your spiritual strength or your sphere of influence, you will find the Christian values in this book pivot on the attributes of God who alone is able to stop anyone from falling. As you read, you will gain guidance to greater heights in life and be able to grasp the concept of the infinite goodness of God.

Bishop (Dr.) Funbi Addo
International Praise Cathedral
Kaduna, Nigeria

The apostle Paul states, *"godliness is profitable for all things, since it holds promise for the present life and also for the life to come"* (1 Tim. 4:8 NASB). *Destined for the Top,* by our brother and friend Joe Ibojie, presents excellent wisdom and revelation to motivate us to a walk of godliness through the enabling and grace of our Lord Jesus Christ who is our sufficiency in all things. God's desire and blessing is that we reach our destiny and maximum potential in our personal lives, relationships, marriage, and family, and in His service for the Kingdom through Christ. Joe's encouragement presented in this book is clearly the fruit of scriptural meditation and a life walked before the Lord over many years. I commend his book as an excellent help toward growing in maturity and toward your God-given destiny.

Steve Boler
Director, School of Prophetic Ministry
Thurso, North of Scotland, UK

Contents

Foreword

*D*ESTINED *for the Top* is a classic must-read for high-profile leadership and aspirants pursuing a next-level balance for gravity, conduct, and longevity of fruitfulness in all spheres of life.

The author of best-sellers, Dr. Joe Ibojie, is a tested and proven pacesetter of values crafted out of an amazing evidence of the inspiration of God in his life. This book has insightful antidotes to lopsided lifestyles. Dr. Ibojie proffers solutions to life's intricate puzzles and answers your most intimate questions including how to get answers to prayers, what steps to take to strengthen marriage and relationships, and how to receive the anointing and maintain righteous living in this modern world.

The well-put-together keys in your hand will catalyze the resolve of any individual or groups to make a positive difference and impact any society in any generation.

Dr. Emmanuel Ziga, President
Grace for All Nations Ministries International
Seattle, Washington

Preface

*D*ESTINED *for the Top* springs forth from the chronicles of life on earth, mostly as they come across our path. It mirrors closely the reflection of the issues that life may throw at us, an indirect tapestry of the challenges—the ups and downs, the failures, and whatever successes that may unravel across the seasons of our lives. It is purposely slanted to reflect real-life struggles, the valley experiences and failures, and the ways God victoriously brings us through them.

As the Psalmist says, *"If the Lord had not been on our side when men attacked us, when their anger flared against us, they would have swallowed us alive"* (Ps. 124:2-3). On my part, I can easily relate to this scenario. I would, therefore, rather glory in weakness so that the excellence may be of His power and not on me, an earthen vessel. I have learned more from observing how my heroes have confronted and risen above the issues that have threatened to cripple their pursuit, rather than from their giftedness. These are the issues of life no one can run from.

Most of the topics covered in this book have accrued from my quiet times with the Lord when the days were not agreeable. They were times of deliberate retreat into the spirit and the periods of silent spiritual warfare. Just as God has said, *"Be still and know that I am God."* Bit by bit, slowly but steadily over the years, storylines often emerge out of the events and circumstances that constitute life on earth. The pages of the memory of our journey will inevitably tell a story and point to an inescapable conclusion: *all of life is spiritual;* by that I mean the things that are visible were conceived and birthed from the unseen world of the supernatural realm. Therefore, those who wait for things to happen before they take reactive action may never be able to influence the course of history. The memories of our days make up the fabric of who we are. As for me, this book indirectly tells the story of how my life has been touched and transformed by God's amazing grace.

> These are the issues of life no one can run from.

Perhaps, like me, you may have had your life turned upside down by what others may consider simple issues. Maybe you have had one or more dreams shattered to pieces despite doing all you knew how to do. Or maybe there have been some mornings when you've lacked the zeal to confront a new day when the future looked bleak and empty. If so, then remember what James said, *"Consider it pure joy, my brothers, whenever you face trials of many kinds"* (James 1:2). Remember also the important and classic statement of the prophet Habakkuk, *"Yet I will rejoice in the Lord, I will be joyful in God my Savior"*

> *Though the fig tree does not bud and there are no grapes on the vines, though the olive crop fails and the fields produce no food, though there are no sheep in the pen and no cattle in the stalls,* ***yet I will rejoice in the Lord, I will be joyful in God my Savior*** (Habakkuk 3:17-18).

In all of life, this is a compelling truth; that after all, if failure isn't a possibility, then success doesn't mean anything. It's for this reason that the Bible says, *"I would have lost heart, unless I had believed that I would see the goodness of the Lord in the land of the living"* (Ps. 27:13 NKJV). A truth in life is that trials and failures will come; but when they do come, we must turn them into opportunities to move forward our lives of purpose.

Life is not a series of mountaintop experiences: even if it were, we are assured that the God of the mountain is the God of the valley; He who rules in the day is also the Lord of the night. Another thing I've learned is that whether circumstances of life attempt to strip everything away from anyone, there is one thing that cannot by taken away—our right of choice.

Ultimately the final outcome in our lives is the sum total of the choices and decisions that we make. My wish is that this book, as you wade through the intricacies of this life, will provide insightful inspirations to sustain and guide you in the right direction.

> If failure isn't a possibility, then success doesn't mean anything.

Unity, love, and sacrifice are prerequisites for living a good life. These important pivots of life also help us to translate personal experiences into good purposes and gains with corporate benefits. How this plays out in real life is like learning to tap into the deeper things of the physical life *and* of the spirit, because life in this physical existence alone is not enough for *"the letter kills but the spirit gives life"* (2 Cor. 3:6).

For one thing, if we want to make the difference and to inform people, we must know that genuine change comes only from the spirit. Hardship will eventually fade from our minds and memory; what will be more lasting is to emerge from tough times with a new and durable confidence in God's amazing love and to gain more insightful knowledge into God's wonderful nature and benevolence and to grasp the concept of the infinite goodness of His universal plan. We may never find answers to all the questions that life poses, but we know that God shapes the entire course of the history to His plan. Truly, as the Bible says, *"My times are in Your hands"* (Ps. 31:15). In all things, God works together for the good of those who love Him, who have been called according to His purpose (see Rom. 8:28).

Whether you are a successful entrepreneur, a pastor of a church, or a full-time housekeeper, you will find that if you, *"live by the Spirit...you will not gratify the desires of the sinful nature"* (Gal. 5:16). I have also correlated spiritual concepts with the mundane things of life on earth to highlight the relevance of spiritual principles in our everyday life.

I am grateful to God for the wonderful family He has given me and for all the people He has placed on my path.

PART I
LIFE ISSUES

Chapter 1

Living by the Rules of Life

The Order of God for a Prosperous, Successful Life

Manoah said, "Now let Your words come to pass! What will be the boy's rule of life, and his work?" (Judges 13:12 NKJV)

To achieve your goals in life, you should know that life has rules.

Manoah received a promise from God in the midst of the collective captivity of Israel and a personal captivity of barrenness. Israel was under a curse from God for disobedience; and on personal level, Manoah's wife was barren. The promise of a son who would begin the deliverance of Israel was therefore a move of God that signaled the end of both captivities. However, Manoah did something that most people neglect to do: He asked for the rules of life for this precious promise.

Every anointing from God comes with its own job description that we must actively seek out. An anointing will not thrive in an "old soul," and an unprepared soul will quench the fire of the new anointing. We must seek the rules of life for the anointing. This consists of personal and corporate aspects, representing guidance for the personal fellowship with God and guidance for corporate fellowship with one another so that the anointing may thrive. Often, the height of our *vertical* relationship with God is dependent on the strength of our *horizontal* fellowship with others.

Rule 1 – Strengthen Your Spirit

The spirit (inner self) is the center of a person and is a spirit that lives in a body and has a soul. From birth, we are taught how to exercise the body, the mind, the will, and emotion, but are never really taught how to exercise the spirit. Yet we are only as strong as our spirit is strong.

Your spirit will give you discernment and will open the door to faith. The Bible says, *"a broken spirit dries the bones"* (Prov. 17:22 NKJV) and that *"by sorrow of the heart the spirit is broken"* (Prov. 15:13 NKJV). Therefore, strengthen your spirit to be able *"to present yourself to God as one approved, a workman who does not need to be ashamed and who correctly handles the word of truth"* (2 Tim. 2:15).

Paul prayed *"that He would grant you, according to the riches of His glory, to be strengthened with might through His Spirit in the inner man"* (Eph. 3:16 NKJV). God often communicates with man through the spirit, *"God is spirit and His worshippers must worship in spirit and in truth"* (John 4:24) for *"Deep calls unto deep at the noise of Your waterfalls…"* (Ps. 42:7 NKJV).

Just as our bodies or natural desires respond to the discipline of our natural father, our spirits also respond to the Father of our spirits:

> *…How much more should we submit to the Father of our spirits and live!* (Hebrews 12:9)

> *For as many as are led by the Spirit of God, these are the sons of God* (Romans 8:14 NKJV).

Whatever happens to the spirit affects the rest of you. On the other hand, the soul is the interaction between the body and the spirit—the medium of interaction, communication between the spirit and the body.

> *Now may the God of peace Himself sanctify you completely; and may your whole spirit, soul, and body be preserved blameless at the coming of our Lord Jesus Christ* (1 Thessalonians 5:23 NKJV).

Rule 2 – The Past Is Not Your Future

You cannot change where you have been, but you *can* influence where you are going—yesterday is gone, tomorrow is yet to come. The joy of life should not only be based on where you have been but also predicated on a cheerful expectation of what lies ahead, and there is so much more to life than just the briefness of yesterday. Reliving the past robs the future and it may even be things that were good or victories of yesterday that you want to continue to relive, as if God is not capable of doing greater things.

As we pass through life, things attach to us by way of memory and tend to keep us emotionally locked up. Often the most difficult are the ones that exist in us and we are not aware of them. Paul said in Galatians 5:1, *"It is for freedom that Christ has set us free. Stand firm then, and do not let yourselves be burdened again by a yoke of slavery."* Anything within us that we cannot control enslaves us. If we are not free of anything and everything that may hinder us, it will show up just at that very moment when God needs us for Himself or His purpose.

> Anything within you that you cannot control enslaves you.

The enemy wants to use the past to steal your power to be free and certain things are hard to leave behind because of the hurt we may have suffered, rightly or wrongly. We therefore need to forgive using release principles. Forgiveness is refreshing water that flows through a once hardened dry valley. As you break through the hold of the past in your life, you will discover God in many areas where you could not previously find Him.

Satan, however, lives in the past. To be effective in his attack on you, he must get you to focus your thinking on your past experiences, particularly the unpleasant ones, and the products of these experiences are usually works of the flesh, envy, jealousy, covetousness, hatred, and unforgiveness.

> Your past is gone, and your today will shape your tomorrow.

However, your past is gone and your today will shape your tomorrow. Your future is in your destiny and our times are in God's hands. Jesus said, *"No one who puts his hand to the plow and looks back is fit for service in the kingdom of God"* (Luke 9:62).

The apostle Paul said:

> *...But one thing I do, forgetting those things which are behind and reaching forward to those things which are ahead, I press toward the goal of the prize of the upward call of God in Christ Jesus* (Philippians 3:13 NKJV).

The Bible also says:

> *Forget the former things; do not dwell on the past. See, I am doing a new thing! Now it springs up; do you not perceive it? I am making a way in the desert and streams in the wasteland* (Isaiah 43:18-19).

Rule 3 – Be Willing to Change

Change is part of life, and whenever you accept that as a fact of life, you will change—you become unsinkable. Change is a process, not an event; and therefore, the results are often not dramatic. It is necessary to realize that if you make up your mind to accept that change is part of life, the transition involved in changing may cause insecurities to emerge, but these will only be temporary.

Change is a sign that something is happening. You should pray that God grants you the serenity to accept the things you cannot change, the courage to change the things you can, and the wisdom to know the difference.[1] Often, true change also comes from the spirit. When times change and people change, the only thing that never changes is the faithfulness of God, and the only thing that is constant is change itself. You can be sure of one thing—change will come! Enjoy today and the people God has placed on your path, for today will never come again, but it will certainly change into yesterday.

Rule 4 – Relationship Is Vital to Human Existence

The basis of our fellowship should be what we mean to each other, not our functions or spiritual gifts; functions may cease, but our love for each other will not fail because love never fails. Rooted deeply in humanity is the need to be loved, understood, and appreciated. The irony is that the measure with which we give it is the same measure with which we receive from God. God loves our diversity, and we are made strong in it because we are designed to need each other. Our differences should not divide us; they are to enhance our lives.

Keep a pure heart: *"Blessed are the pure in heart, for they will see God"* (Matt. 5:8). The Bible also says, *"To the pure, all things are pure, but to those who are corrupted and do not believe, nothing is pure. In fact, both their minds and consciences are corrupted"* (Titus 1:15).

Rule 5 – Invest in Your Potential

Identify your passion and invest in it. The key to your breakthrough is to dig deep into the deposits of God in your life and maximize the circumstance. Do not dwell too long on what you do not have. Instead, give time to developing what you *do* have. Within the midst of you there are blessings that contain the seed for your tomorrow.

Rule 6 – Be Prepared to Make Sacrifices

Sacrifice is the forfeiture of something highly valued for the sake of something considered greater. It means giving up something that you may attain something else. This is what King David said to Araunah, *"No, I insist on paying the full price. I will not take for the Lord what is yours, or sacrifice a burnt offering that costs me nothing"* (1 Chron. 21:24).

Making sacrifices is essential in our walk with God. Often there is a cost associated with sacrifice. It is this cost that determines the value of the sacrifice. Among the many types of sacrifice that exist, three types stand out and are worth note—the sacrifice of praise, service, and worship.

Praise—*"Through Jesus, therefore, let us continually offer to God a sacrifice of praise—the fruit of lips that confess His name"* (Heb. 13:15). **Service**—*"And do not forget to do good and to share with others, for with such sacrifices God is pleased"* (Heb. 13:16). **Worship**—*"Therefore, I urge you, brothers, in view of God's mercy, to offer your bodies as living sacrifices, holy and pleasing to God—this is your spiritual act of worship"* (Rom.

12:1). We were made to fellowship and worship Him, *"Gather to Me My consecrated ones, who made a covenant with Me by sacrifice"* (Ps. 50:5).

Rule 7 – Know that Feelings are Fickle

Do not rely on your feelings; depend on the Word of God to sharpen your spiritual discernment instead. With spiritual discernment, you can discern the real reason or spirit behind an outward manifestation. Your spirit bears witness with the Spirit of God.

On the contrary, the enemy can contaminate your mind, affect your will, and dictate your emotions—the enemy is, therefore, after your soul. Whoever controls your soul will control your experiences in life and eventually your destiny. Remember, Eve did not mean to harm Adam; her feelings just got the better of her. God is mindful of your thought process: your soul is quite important and if strong can control your body; together the soul and the body can run in mutiny against the rule of the spirit. Remember, as a people think in their hearts, so they are—and no one can rise above the limit of his or her imagination.

Rule 8 – The Power of Obedience

The prophet Samuel made the power of obedience clear when he admonished Saul:

> *Samuel replied, "Does the Lord delight in burnt offerings and sacrifices as much as in obeying the voice of the Lord? To obey is better than sacrifice, and to heed is better than the fat of rams* (1 Samuel 15:22).

> *If you are willing and obedient, you will eat the best from the land; but if you resist and rebel, you will be devoured by the sword. For the mouth of the Lord has spoken* (Isaiah 1:19-20).

Obedience is no obedience when it is not complete, so we should avoid partial obedience. As James 2:10 says, *"For whoever keeps the whole law and yet stumbles at just one point is guilty of breaking all of it."*

Rule 9 – Avoid the Danger of Worldly Ambition

Ambition means the eagerness or strong desire to achieve success at something. It is not a bad thing, but pursuing a vision without godliness compromises the virtue of ambition and it then becomes worldly ambition. However, the Bible says that without vision people perish, so there is a need for the delicate balancing of these two extremes (see Prov. 29:18).

Attaining your goal with godliness is essential and is referred to as godly ambition. Also, ambition and contentment often appear as the opposite poles of the same measurements, so contentment without godliness is therefore a reproach while godliness with contentment is a great gain: *"But godliness with contentment is great gain"* (1 Tim. 6:6). If you have godly contentment, God will tell you when to advance just as He did with the Israelites in their wilderness experience. *"... You have stayed long enough at this mountain. Break camp and advance..."* (Deut. 1:6-7). Contentment is a lack of desire for more than what you have and is only virtuous if guarded by godliness. Without this godliness, contentment may be tantamount to idleness.

> The opposite of godly ambition is inordinate ambition.

The opposite of godly ambition is inordinate ambition. This is the unrestrained desire to achieve success by exceeding reason or limits. Lucifer had inordinate ambitions to be like God and this led to his downfall. Absalom also had inordinate ambition when he conspired against King David and failed. This kind of ambition began in the Garden of Eden:

*"You will not surely die," the serpent said to the woman. "For God knows that when you eat of it your eyes will be opened, and **you will be like God**, knowing good and evil." When the woman saw that the fruit of the tree was good for food and pleasing to the eye, and also desirable for gaining wisdom, she took some and ate it. She also gave some to her husband, who was with her, and he ate it"* (Genesis 3:4-6).

Two Examples of Worldly Ambition

1. *Now the whole world had one language and a common speech. As men moved eastward, they found a plain in Shinar and settled there. They said to each other, "Come, let's make bricks and bake them thoroughly" They used brick instead of stone, and tar for mortar. Then they said, **"Come, let us build ourselves a city, with a tower that reaches to the heavens, so that we may make a name for ourselves** and not be scattered over the face of the whole earth." But the Lord came down to see the city and the tower that the men were building. The Lord said, "If as one people speaking the same language they have begun to do this, then nothing they plan to do will be impossible for them* (Genesis 11:1-6).

The lessons and the characteristics of worldly ambition in this story are:

- Inordinate ambition
- Self-centeredness
- Vain glory
- Self-exaltation
- No regard to the will of God

2. *In the course of time, Absalom provided himself with a chariot and horses and with fifty men to run ahead of him. He would get up early and stand by the side of the road leading to the city gate. Whenever anyone came with a complaint to be placed before the king for a decision, Absalom would call out to him, "Which town are you from?" He would answer, "Your servant is from one of the tribes of Israel." Then Absalom would say to him, "Look, your claims are valid and proper, but there is no representative of the king to hear you." And Absalom would add, "If only I were appointed judge in the land! Then everyone who has a complaint or case could come to me and I would see that he receives justice." Also, whenever anyone approached him to bow down before him, Absalom would reach out his hand, take hold of him*

*and kiss him. Absalom behaved in this way toward all the Israelites who came to the king asking for justice, and **so he stole the hearts of the men of Israel*** (2 Samuel 15:1-6).

The lessons and further characteristics of worldly ambition in this story are:

- Pretentiousness
- Deception
- Being manipulative
- Disloyalty to the existing authority
- Stealing the hearts of people by manipulation
- Being overbearing

The Bible is quite clear on how far we need to take our ambition so that we do not become worldly in our pursuits and also how not to become victims of slothfulness in contentment without godliness. *"In his heart a man plans his course, but the Lord determines* [directs] *his steps"* (Prov. 16:9). This means that we need to have our plans but also to be open to God's intervention at all times. That is why the Bible says, "Man proposes, God disposes" (see Prov. 19:21).

Here are some more Bible verses on this topic:

Commit to the Lord whatever you do, and your plans will succeed (Proverbs 16:3).

Trust in the Lord with all your heart and lean not on your own understanding; in all your ways acknowledge Him, and He will make your paths straight (Proverbs 3:5-6).

Make it your ambition to lead a quiet life, to mind your own business and to work with your hands, just as we told you, so that your daily life may win the respect of outsiders and so that you will not be dependent on anybody (1 Thessalonians 4:11-12).

Endnote

1. The Serenity Prayer, well-known prayer thought to be written by American theologian Reinhold Niebuhr in the late 1930s.

DESTINY DELIBERATIONS

1. "Every anointing from God comes with its own job description that we must actively seek out."

    Question: Throughout the years, have you sought out your God-given job description and received your anointing?

    _____

    _____

    Question: Are you currently fulfilling your job description responsibilities?

    _____

    _____

2. "Identify your passion and invest in it."

    Question: Have you identified your passion and have you invested in it?

    _____

    _____

    Question: For instance, if you enjoy working on the computer, singing, or helping people, have you taken classes to enhance your knowledge and skills?

    _____

    _____

    Question: Do you believe that investing in yourself will move you toward fulfilling your potential?

    _____

    _____

3. "Attaining your goal with godliness is essential and is referred to as godly ambition." Having a God-given goal brings purpose and meaning to life.

    Question: Are you working and aiming toward attaining your goals (and dreams) with godly ambition?

    _____

    _____

Chapter 2

Living by Love

*Be imitators of God, therefore, as dearly loved children **and live a life of love,** just as Christ loved us and gave Himself up for us as a fragrant offering and sacrifice to God* (Ephesians 5:1-2).

O NE of the hallmarks of a true disciple of Jesus is living by love so that all people can read the testimony of your life. Without love, you live in darkness; and when there is darkness within a person, it is almost impossible to navigate to your destiny.

The key to the measure of all fullness in God is love. It is very important that we are not ignorant of this fact: *"Whoever does not love does not know God, because God is love"* (1 John 4:8). Love is pivotal to the relational and covenant-keeping attributes of God. Whoever lives in love, lives in God and God in him.

Love and a reverent fear of God are connected. To fear God is to worship, respect, and love Him enough to desire to do what is right—no matter what. In reality, to love God is to never get weary of doing even the smallest thing for Him. God is not so much impressed with the dimension or magnitude of the work we do as He is with the love in which it is done. If we love God, we will find obeying His commandments easy. We should commit our basic resources of time, talents, and treasures to God. Where your treasure is, there your heart is also (see Matt. 6:21).

The basis of our fellowship is not on our giftedness, but on what we mean to each other. Gifts may fail, but love never fails. Paul said, *"But eagerly desires the greatest gifts. And now I will show you the most excellent way"* (1 Cor. 12:31). This "most excellent way" that Paul refers to is love. The escape route out of any predicament is to practice the love of God.

> True love never fails.

Paul also said, *"If I speak in the tongues of men and of angels, but have not love, I am only a resounding gong or a clanging cymbal..."* Of the three great virtues of life, Paul says in the same passage, *"And now these three remain: faith, hope and love, the greatest of these is **love**"* (1 Cor. 13:1-13).

The spirit of love comes from God, *"...the love of God has been poured out in our hearts by the Holy Spirit who was given to us"* (Rom. 5:5 NKJV). The Bible also says, *"A new command I give you: Love one another. As I have loved you, so you must love one another. By this all men will know that you are My disciples, if you love one another"* (John 13:34-35).

We are not born with the spirit of love in our hearts. In the Book of Jeremiah, the Bible says, *"the heart is deceitful above all things and desperately wicked; who can know it?"* (Jer. 17:9 NKJV). In Genesis 8:21 God said, *"Never again will I curse the ground because of man, even though every inclination of his heart is evil from childhood."* By natural inclination, humankind's heart is wicked. Such a heart is set on the flesh, which is *"hostile to God. It does not submit itself to God's law, nor can it do so"* (Rom. 8:6-7).

We love because God first loved us. God said, *"I will give you a new heart and put a new spirit in you; I will remove from you your heart of stone and give you a heart of flesh"* (Ezek. 36:26). The onus, therefore, rests on us to practice living by love. The natural self, the unregenerate soul, is a God-hater and lives in rebellion, but Christians are filled with the Spirit of God. The Bible says, *"For as many as are led by the Spirit of God, these are sons of God"* (Rom. 8:14 NKJV).

> The natural inclination of humanity's heart is evil.

Truly, *"How great is the love the Father has lavished on us, that we should be called children of God!..."* (1 John 3:1).

The Dynamics of Love

The Bible gives an excellent description of the dynamics of love in a very practical way:

> *Love must be sincere. Hate what is evil; cling to what is good. Be devoted to one another in brotherly love. Honor one another above yourselves. Never be lacking in zeal, but keep your spiritual fervor, serving the Lord. Be joyful in hope, patient in affliction, faithful in prayer. Share with God's people who are in need. Practice hospitality.*
>
> *Bless those who persecute you; bless and do not curse. Rejoice with those who rejoice; mourn with those who mourn. Live in harmony with one another. Do not be proud, but be willing to associate with people of low position. Do not be conceited. Do not repay anyone evil for evil. Be careful to do what is right in the eyes of everybody. If it is possible, as far as it depends on you, live at peace with everyone. Do not take revenge,*

> *my friends, but leave room for God's wrath, for it is written, "It is Mine to avenge; I will repay" says the Lord.*
>
> *On the contrary, "If your enemy is hungry, feed him; if he is thirsty, give him something to drink. In doing this, you will heap burning coals on his head." Do not be overcome by evil, but overcome evil with good* (Romans 12:9-21).

This Scripture passage expresses the true dynamics of the practicality of love.

Love is the summation of all the commandments. The Bible also says that love is the epitome and the coming together of all the laws of God:

> **Love is the summation of all the commandments.**

> *Let no debt remain outstanding, except the continuing debt to love one another, for he who loves his fellowman has fulfilled the law. The commandments, "Do not commit adultery," "Do not murder," "Do not steal," "Do not covet," and whatever other commandment there may be, are summed up in this one rule: "Love your neighbor as yourself." Love does no harm to its neighbor.* **Therefore love is the fulfillment of the law.**

And do this, understanding the present time. The hour has come for you to wake up from your slumber, because our salvation is nearer now than when we first believed. The night is nearly over; the day is almost here. So let us put aside the deeds of darkness and put on the armor of light. Let us behave decently, as in the daytime, not in the orgies and drunkenness, not in sexual immorality and debauchery, not in dissension and jealousy. Rather, clothe yourselves with the Lord Jesus Christ, and do not think about how to gratify the desires of the sinful nature (Romans 13:8-14).

This is the essence of love.

The practical aspect of love is putting this scriptural injunctions concerning love into practice in our lives. No one can impact or significantly influence another person without first showing compassion or doing it out of love. In the spirit realm, compassion and love always precede the miraculous. This is particularly applicable within the context of living by love in a marriage situation. There is a correlation between the practice of love, lack of sin, goodness, and forgiveness. However, lack of sin is not equivalent to goodness, for goodness is more than freedom from sin. In practical terms, goodness is holiness put into practice.

Holiness comprises of freedom from sin, being consecrated to God and living according to a divine spiritual system of purpose. Love, on the other hand, transcends even the borders of goodness for it entails sacrifice and selflessness in a manner that goes deeper than goodness. *"Greater love has no one than this, that he lay down his life for his friends"* (John 15:13). Indeed, there is no greater love!

> Goodness is holiness put into practice.

> *If anyone says, "I love God" yet hates his brother, he is a liar. For anyone who does not love his brother, whom he has seen, cannot love God, whom he has not seen. And He has given us this command: Whoever loves God must also love his brother* (1 John 4:21).

I have observed that the extent to which we live in love correlates with the expression of our spirituality. In accordance with the love of God that dwells in a person, there are three levels of spiritual existence in which the person can live. He can either live by the sinful nature that is without the love of God or live by the spirit of love, which comes from God. However, many people live in between these two levels. Sadly, most

Christians are in this category, oscillating between the desires of their sinful nature and the desires of the Spirit of God.

The three levels are:

1. The Middle Level — Middle level people are described as babes in Christ. Though they know of the love of God, they allow themselves to be pulled in and out of obedience to God. They have tendencies to sin and often allow the progeny of their darker days or their pre-Christian lives to continue to crown the throne of their lives. The apostle Paul described this category very well when he said:

    Brothers, I could not address you as spiritual but as worldly—mere infants in Christ. I gave you milk to drink, not solid food, for you were not ready for it. Indeed, you are still not ready. You are still worldly. For since there is jealousy and quarreling among you, are you not worldly? Are you not acting like mere men? (1 Corinthians 3:1-3)

    According to Paul they fluctuate between wild natural tendencies and life in the spirit.

2. The Natural Self — The natural self is inclined to operating without the love of God. This is the lowest level of spiritual existence. This person does

not understand nor accept the things of the spirit and does not know God, having no desire, no fear, and no reverence for God. This person is disobedient to God, has no faith, and he resists the truth of God. People like this are far away from God and enemies of God. They live lives dominated by sinful desires, wickedness, and vile and devilish things; anything that feels good goes. The natural self heads for eternal separation from God unless he or she receives redemption by faith through the atoning blood of Jesus Christ.

3. The Spiritual Self — The spiritual self is motivated by the love of God. This is the highest level of our existence and is the level where God intended all people to live. The spiritual self accepts Jesus Christ, walks by godly wisdom, accepts the Word of God, and desires the truths of God. This is the safest level to be in: To do what is holy by putting goodness into practice and by being righteous in the eyes of God. The spiritual self lives in the shelter of Almighty God, shares the confidence that comes from faith of God, and is as bold as a lion.

The Reward of Living by Love

There is great reward in practicing how to live by love, and the Bible is replete with such instances. If we remain in love, we will rise above our circumstances. As the Bible says:

> *Who shall separate us from the love of Christ? Shall trouble or hardship or persecution or famine or nakedness or danger or sword? No, in all these things we are more than conquerors through Him who loved us* (Romans 8:35,37).

There is power in living by love and an even more formidable power exudes from the love of Christ for us. God Himself works on the behalf of those who live by love and keep His covenant. The apostle Paul said, *"And we know that in all things God works for good for those who love Him, who have been called according to His purpose"* (Rom. 8:28).

Daniel and Nehemiah also agreed that God keeps His covenant of love with those who love Him: *"O Lord, God of heaven, the great and awesome God, who keeps His covenant of love with those who love Him and obey His commands"* (Neh. 1:5; see Dan. 9:4). God said to them, *"I will not violate My covenant…"* (Ps. 89:34). Aside from this, there is also a better relational value in living by love, because love covers a multitude of faults (see 1 Pet. 4:8).

The First and Greatest Commandment

Jesus said:

> *Love the Lord your God with all your heart and will all your soul and with your entire mind and with all your strength. This is the first and greatest commandment. And the second is like it: Love your neighbor as yourself. All the Law and the Prophets hang on these two commandments* (Matthew 22:37-40).

Here, God emphasized that the entire law and the prophets of God hang on the practice of living by love. The irony of life is that the greatest atrocities committed against humanity are traceable to those who, by reason of unpleasant life experiences, have lost their capacity to love themselves, therefore rendering themselves unable to love others.

Responsiveness to the Call of God

I have also observed that there appears to be a correlation between love and responsiveness to the call of God.

The degree to which you live by love is related to your responsiveness to the call of God in your life. You can correlate the levels of love with personal sacrifice and the calling of God in life.

Love with	Sacrifice	Calling of God
Heart	**Of obedience**	**Salvation**
(Loving with the heart leads to the sacrifice of obedience)	1 Peter 2:4 Romans 12:1	Romans 10:10 *(Sacrifice of obedience creates the way to salvation)*
Soul	**Of praise**	**Sanctification**
(Loving with the soul leads to the sacrifice of praise and worship)	Hebrews 13:15 Psalm 50:13-14	Hebrews 13:12 *(Praise & worship enhance the way to sanctification)*
Strength	**Of service**	**Service**
(Loving with strength leads to the sacrifice of service)	Hebrews 13:16 Philippians 4:18	Philippians 4:19 *(With sacrifice of service comes the call of God to His service)*

Loving with the heart leads to the sacrifice of obedience, of which the first call of God is to salvation. Loving with the soul leads to the sacrifice of praise and worship, which comes with the call of God to sanctification. Loving with strength leads to the sacrifice of service; and with it, the call of God to His service.

The Power of Love

Like Paul, I:

> *...pray that you, being rooted and established in love, may have power, together with all saints, to grasp how wide and long and high and deep is the love of Christ, and to know this love that surpasses knowledge—that you may be filled to the measure of all the fullness of God* (Ephesians 3:17-19).

No one can tap into the true measure of the fullness of God's power without the love of God.

Love and Forgiveness

Love and forgiveness are intricately interwoven. Forgiveness is the cornerstone of Christianity. The kingdom of Heaven was founded on the forgiveness that comes from the cross. The cross is the emblem of human unfairness, wickedness, and disobedience and also the all-surpassing love of God for humanity, *"Therefore I say to you, her sins, which are many, are forgiven, for she loved much. But to whom little is forgiven, the same loves little"* (Luke 7:47 NKJV).

Forgiveness is an act of love and is connected to living by faith. Jesus said:

> *So watch yourselves, if your brother sins, rebuke him, and if he repents, forgive him. If he sins against you seven times in a day, and seven times comes back to you and says, "I repent," forgive him. The apostles said to the Lord, "Increase our faith!"* (Luke 17:3-5).

Being unforgiving is an act of wickedness.

So, the degree to which you are able to forgive is a reflection of your faith in God and His love in your life.

Jesus Christ made it clear that being unforgiving is an act of wickedness:

> *Therefore, the kingdom of heaven is like a king who wanted to settle accounts with his servants. As he began the settlement, a man who owed him ten thousand talents was brought to him. Since he was not able to pay, the master ordered*

that he and his wife and children and all that he had be sold to repay the debt.

The servant fell on his knees before him. "Be patient with me," he begged, "and I will pay back everything." The servant's master took pity on him, cancelled the debt and let him go.

But when that servant went out, he found one of his fellow servants who owed him a hundred denari. He grabbed him and began to choke him. "Pay back what you owe me!" he demanded.

His fellow servant fell to his knees and begged him, "Be patient with me, and I will pay you back." But he refused. Instead, he went off and had the man thrown into prison until he could pay the debt. When the other servants saw what had happened, they were greatly distressed and went and told their master everything that had happened.

Then the master called the servant in. **"You wicked servant,"** he said, "I cancelled all that debt of yours because you begged me to. Shouldn't you have had mercy on your fellow-servant just as I had on you?" In anger his master turned him over to the jailers to be tortured, until he should pay back all he owed.

This is how My heavenly Father will treat each of you unless you forgive your brother from your heart (Matthew 18:23-35).

In this parable, Jesus called the servant wicked and unforgiving; he was handed over to the jailers to be locked up. This spirit behind unforgiveness locks up people in a sea of anger, bitterness, and hatred toward others. The state of being locked up in the spirit amounts to going to prison where guilt, depression, frustration, pain, and anxieties act as tormentors and work their havoc without restriction.

Forgiveness works on the release principle. First, one has to release the person who committed the perceived wrongful act, and this forgiveness releases the power of love, which is capable of setting anyone free.

Unforgiveness opens you up to the bitterness, hatred, and cruelty of these wicked tormentors. It also takes away the shield of protection from the Lord, and the pains of unforgiveness go beyond the level of the pains of the wrongful act. Instead, it embodies the agony of the hurt inflicted by the tormentors.

Forgiveness also works on a reciprocal principle. *"If you do not forgive men their sins, your Father will not forgive your sins"* (Matt. 6:15). The measure with which you give is the same measure with which you will receive. The love of God is uncon-

> Forgiveness is an act of grace, not a reward for good behavior.

ditional, but His forgiveness is conditional and proportional to how we forgive others.

Forgiveness is an act of grace, not a reward for good behavior, so we should not forgive because of our own agenda. This is why the Lord Jesus Christ asks us to forgive others seventy times seven times if the need arises: Freely we have received and freely we should give. The acid test for spiritual maturity is therefore how we love and forgive others.

DESTINY DELIBERATIONS

1. "By natural inclination, humankind's heart is wicked. Such a heart is set on the flesh, which is hostile to God."

    Question: How hard is it to keep your heart from seeking other than godly things to do, to think about, to feel, and to love?

    _____

    _____

2. "Love and forgiveness are intricately interwoven. Forgiveness is the cornerstone of Christianity."

    Question: Is forgiveness the cornerstone of your attitude toward those who hurt you?

    _____

    _____

Question: How intricately interwoven are love and for-giveness in your overall outlook on life?

_____

_____

3. "The love of God is unconditional, but His forgiveness is conditional and proportional to how we forgive others."

Question: Is this statement comforting or a bit alarm-ing? Why?

_____

_____

Chapter 3

Living in Unity

The Power of Unity
Together we can make a difference.

How good and pleasant it is when brothers live together in unity! It is like precious oil poured on the head, running down on the beard, running down on Aaron's beard, down upon the collar of his robes. It is as if the dew of Hermon were falling on Mount Zion, for there the LORD bestows His blessing, even life for evermore (Psalm 133:1-3).

SOLOMON'S prayer in Second Chronicles 6 marks a high point in the unity of Israel as a nation. With one mind, one spirit, and one heart, the nation came together in worship at the glittering new temple; and the supernatural coexistence, the unseen realm of God, became visible to mere mortals. The result was a display of the awesome power of God. They saw the fire of God come down from Heaven and the glory of the Lord in the form of a dark cloud filled the temple:

> *The priests could not enter the temple of the Lord because the glory of the Lord filled it. When all the Israelites saw the fire coming down and the glory of the Lord above the temple, they knelt on the pavement with their faces to the ground and they worshipped and gave thanks to the Lord saying "He is good; His love endures forever* (2 Chronicles 7:2-3).

In the New Testament, the Book of the Acts of the Apostles also records a similar occurrence:

> *When the day of Pentecost came, they were all together in one place. Suddenly a sound like the bowing of a violent wind came from heaven and filled the whole house where they were sitting. They saw what seemed to be tongues of fire that separated and came to rest on each of them. All of them were filled with the Holy Spirit and began to speak in other tongues as the Holy Spirit enabled them* (Acts 2:1-4).

Onlookers *"heard this sound, a crowd came together in bewilderment"* (v. 6) and were so *"amazed and perplexed, they asked one another, 'What does this mean?'"* (v. 12). *"Then Peter stood up with the Eleven, raised his voice, and addressed the crowd"* (v. 14). *"When the people heard this, they were cut to the heart and said to Peter and the other apostles, 'Brothers, what shall we do?'"* (v. 37). Notice here, that the Bible says, Peter stood up with the Eleven and raised his voice. Peter's voice became more influential because he was in unity with the other eleven disciples. The impartation of Peter's speech was propelled by the weight of their unity as they stood in one accord and one purpose. Of course the heavens responded. And as always, when the Holy Spirit moves and manifests the majesty of God, people respond.

Where Are His Wonders Today?

You may ask in the words of Gideon, *"Where are all His wonders that our fathers told us about...?"* (Judg. 6:13). The gospel has not lost its power: it is the power of God unto salvation. In most cases, the inability of our present generation to come to genuine unity, whether at the level of the local church or at a national level, has left us with only a few signs accompanying the preaching of the Word. These occasional signs and wonders are often celebrated, but in reality they are just glimpses of what the Lord wants to give us. When the real seal of approval comes from Heaven in the fullness of God, He will speak for Himself.

These glorious manifestations of His presence teach us many things; but most importantly, they teach us that it is time to lay aside those things that divide us and practice instead the things that lead to mutual edification and peace. For the Bible says how pleasant it is when brethren dwell together in unity and it's there that God commands His blessing (see Ps. 133:1). The blessing of God is the power to obtain the desired results.

> Power comes when we are united in purpose, mind, and heart.

Even now, I dare say these glorious manifestations can and do happen in our time! They are not incredible when viewed from God's perspective. Like the Bible says, *"Why should any of you consider it incredible that God raises the dead?"* (Acts 26:8). These things can happen again! We can make the difference if we cry out, *"O Lord, revive Your work in the midst of the years! In the midst of the years make it known..."* (Hab. 3:2 NKJV). Power comes when we are united in purpose, mind, and heart. Again, in Acts 4:24 *"They raised their voices together,"* and the Lord answered with an earthquake. The point is found in raising many voices together, for it shows the beauty and power of diversity coming together, and that there are certain spheres of the spiritual realm that we can only penetrate if we are in unity.

The writer of Hebrews echoed this when he said, *"Therefore let us leave the elementary teachings about Christ and go on to maturity..."* (Heb. 6:1). To continue with division along the lines of doctrinal principles, such as baptism and of the laying on of hands, drags us away from the crux of the matter. Those who perpetuate such division are mere infants who require spiritual milk and not solid food, for solid food is for the mature. What does *"solid food"* mean? *"Love your enemies, bless those who curse you, do good for those who hate you and pray for those who spitefully use and persecute you"* (Matt. 5:44 NKJV). Solid food is deep teaching of God meant for those who are mature in Christ.

Friction and Brotherly Love

When friction appears, it's usually a sign of alignment of different parts of the Body of Christ rather than the signs of rancor. Therefore, we must approach friction in the Body with a positive attitude and see it as the blending of various gifts. After all, as a family of believers, we should realize that kindred feuding is not new. From Cain and Abel of *"Am I my brother's keeper?"* (Gen. 4:9) through to Peter and John of *"Lord, what about him?"* (John 21:21), even to this day it thrives.

What counts is where you will be when all the dust settles, and remember that brotherly love is the acid test of true spiritual maturity. You may pick and choose friends and neighbors, but God chooses your brothers. Someday God is going to ask, *"Where is your brother?"* And depending on your answer, He will probably say to you *"What have you done?"* Therefore, overcome your differences, and keep your brothers.

For David, the test of brotherly love came from Saul, and for Joseph it was his blood brothers. Both men overcame their kindred struggles but retained their covenant of brotherhood and their relationship with God; otherwise they would have lost the Father's favor.

Some of life's situations are divinely set up, and we must be careful to discern the true reason for each of our life experiences. Often they may have been orchestrated to bring us to the next move of God in our lives. So we must confront the issues as they come, in uprightness and humility, and keep the biblical injunction that says, *"Let brotherly love continue"* (Heb. 13:1 NKJV), no matter what happens. Remember what Jesus said, *"By this all men will know that you are My disciples, if you love each other"* (John 13:35).

We need to realize that God presents great chances camouflaged in small packages. As mortals, we often do not know when we stand at the precipice of history. Such opportunities don't come with pomp or pageantry, just as the Bible asks, *"Who despises the days of the small things?"* (Zech. 4:10).

The common interest of everyone should be paramount in our hearts at all times, and we should flee from parochialism and self-centeredness. Consider this touching story: Ensconced in the safety and luxury of the palace of the powerful Persian Empire was the lonely voice of Esther, a lady of Jewish descent. At the risk of her life, she laid aside personal comfort and security to save the Jewish race. Her courageous words are now a classic statement of heroism among those who put the interests of others before self. She said:

> *Go, gather all the Jews who are present in Susa, and fast for me. Do not eat or drink for three days, night or day. I and my maids will fast as you do. When this is done, I will go to the king, even though it is against the law. And if I perish, I perish* (Esther 4:16).

The profile of this sacrifice stands out for all time. Mordecai must have had good foresight when he said to her, *"And who knows but that you have come to royal position for such a time as this?"* (Esther 4:14).

This challenge was a wakeup call for her and it is as relevant now as it was then.

> The common interest of everyone should be paramount in our hearts at all times.

Like Esther, we need each other to fulfill our purpose in life. Esther needed Mordecai to come to a place of boldness. A tree does not make a forest. No matter how big it may be. Even the eagle in all its abilities needs a push to bring out its best. There are several things we could accomplish in our lives but, in the midst of all that surrounds us, there is always a central purpose, and a cause for which to live. Jesus put this better than mere mortals could ever put it, *"For this cause I was born"* (John 18:37 NKJV). My prayer to you is that, just as it was said of David, you will not die until you have *"served God's purpose in* [your] *own generation"* (Acts 13:36). This is what counts.

The Power of Unity

In the Book of Acts of the Apostles, there are many instances when the power of the unity was displayed to the view of all present. In Acts 4 we read in verse 24: *"When they heard this, they raised their voices together in prayer to God."* And God replied with an earthquake that shook the place where they were.

> *After they prayed, the place where they were meeting was shaken, and they were all filled with the Holy Spirit and spoke the word of God boldly* (Acts 4:31).

Even the first Pentecostal experience on earth was heralded by the power of unity; the Bible says that they were all with one accord in one place.

> *When the day of Pentecost came, they were all together in one place. Suddenly a sound like the blowing of a violent wind came from heaven and filled the whole house where they were sitting. They saw what seemed to be tongues of fire that separated and came to reset on each of them. All of them were filled with the Holy Spirit and began to speak in other tongues as the Spirit enabled them* (Acts 2:1-4).

> How easily we connect with Heaven when we are united.

Notice that the sound came from Heaven. How easily we connect with Heaven when we are united. Even before the tongues of fire separated and came to rest on each person, the Holy Spirit first filled the room in which they stayed on that day; ordinary men were transformed and empowered with extraordinary abilities.

James was killed at the command of Herod, and since it pleased the Jews, he proceeded to arrest Peter with the intention of also killing him after the Easter festivities. But the church came together and prayed. God sent an angel to release

Peter, the Iron Gate opened on its own, and it happened so miraculously that Peter thought he was dreaming even before the church had finished their prayers.

> *So Peter was kept in prison, but the church was earnestly praying to God for him. The night before Herod was to bring him to trial, Peter was sleeping between two soldiers, bound with two chains, and sentries stood guard at the entrance. Suddenly an angel of the Lord appeared and a light shone in the cell. He struck Peter on the side and woke him up. "Quick, get up!" he said, and the chains fell off Peter's wrists.*

> *Then the angel said to him, "Put on your clothes and sandals" And Peter did so. "Wrap your cloak around you and follow me," the angel told him. Peter followed him out of the prison but he had no idea that what the angel was doing was really happening; he thought he was seeing a vision. They passed the first and second guards and came to the Iron Gate leading to the city. It opened for them by itself, and they went through it. When they had walked the length of one street suddenly the angel left him.*

> *Then Peter came to himself and said "Now I
> know without a doubt that the Lord sent His
> angel and rescued me from Herod's clutches and
> from everything the Jewish people were antici-
> pating." When this had dawned on him, he went
> to the house of Mary the mother of John, also
> called Mark, where many people had gathered
> and were praying* (Acts 12:5-12).

Nehemiah was truly a man of outstanding character, his strategy for rebuilding the walls of Jerusalem was classic; each man rebuilt the wall in front of his house. In no time a great amount of the wall was rebuilt. There is no telling how much we can achieve when we work in unity.

> *The men of Jericho rebuilt the adjoining section,
> and Zacuur, son of Imri, built next to them. The
> Fish Gate was rebuilt by the sons of Hassenaah.
> They laid its beams and put on its doors and
> bolts, while Meshullam, son of Berekiah, the son
> of Meshezabel, made repairs, and next to him
> Zadok, son of Baana, also made repairs. The
> next section was repaired by the men of Tekoa,
> but their nobles would not put their shoulders
> to work under their supervisors* (Nehemiah
> 3:2-5).

When Joshua was at war with the Amalekites, Moses went to the mountaintop to pray to God with his staff raised toward Heaven, but soon his hand got weary and tired. Then something remarkable happened. Joshua, who was previously triumphing over the Amalekites, started to suffer defeat. Joshua lost the momentum of the war. Moses' symbolic act of raising his hands in prayer was connected to Joshua's success in the faraway battle. So Hur and Aaron came to support Moses' hands, and Joshua again gained the upper hand and won the victory against the Amalekites because of this wonderful spiritual chain of responsibilities. This is how the Bible puts it:

> *The Amalekites came out and attacked the Israelites at Rephidim. Moses said to Joshua, "Choose some of our men and go out to fight the Amalekites. Tomorrow I will stand on the top of the hill with the staff of God in my hands." So Joshua fought the Amalekites as Moses had ordered, and Moses, Aaron and Hur went to the top of the hill. As long as Moses held up his hands, the Israelites were winning but whenever he lowered his hands the Amalekites were winning, when Moses' hands grew tired, they took a stone and put it under him and he sat on it. Aaron and Hur held his hands up—one on one side and one on the other—so that his hands*

remained steady till sunset, so Joshua overcame the Amalekite army with the sword (Exodus 17:8-13).

There are certain levels of spiritual advancement that can only be achieved by the power of unity and this will happen only if we come together.

DESTINY DELIBERATIONS

1. "With one mind, one spirit, and one heart, the nation came together...."

   Question: Do you see this scenario happening in your family, your church, your community, or your nation? Why or why not?

   _____

   _____

   Question: What steps can you take to move toward this happening?

   _____

   _____

2. "We need to realize that God presents great chances camouflaged in small packages."

   Question: Is your mind, spirit, and heart open to recognize and receive God's opportunities—big or small?

   _____

   _____

3. "How easily we connect with Heaven when we are united."

   Question: Have you experienced Heaven during corporate prayer or another activity?

   _____

   _____

   Question: What was it like? If you haven't, write what you think it is like to connect with Heaven.

   _____

   _____

Chapter 4

Living Wisely

Do you want to be counted wise, to build a rep-
utation for wisdom? Here's what you do: Live
well, live wisely, live humbly. It's the way you
live, not the way you talk, that counts (James
3:13 The Message).

THE Bible makes it abundantly clear that the source of
spiritual wisdom is not philosophy, but Jesus Christ;
therefore, spiritual wisdom is Christ and Him crucified. The
Bible speaks clearly of this:

> *My purpose is that they may be encouraged*
> *in heart and united in love, so that they may*
> *have the full riches of complete understand-*
> *ing, in order that they may know the mystery*
> *of God, namely, Christ, in whom are hidden all*

> *the treasures of wisdom and knowledge. I tell*
> *you this so that no one may deceive you by fine-*
> *sounding arguments* (Colossians 2:2-4).

It is impossible to obtain spiritual wisdom and knowledge without knowing Christ—and Christ crucified (see 1 Cor. 2:2). When we know Christ, we receive all the treasures of the wisdom and knowledge that are hidden in Him. Therefore, to know Jesus Christ is to know everything we will ever need in life. That is living by the wisdom of God.

There are two kinds of wisdom: wisdom of this world and wisdom from Heaven. The wisdom from God is the practical application of the Word of God in our lives. That is why James 3:13 says, *"Who is wise and understanding among you? Let him show it by his good life, by deeds done in humility that comes from wisdom."*

This is how The Message Bible translation puts it:

> *Do you want to be counted wise, to build a repu-*
> *tation for wisdom? Here's what you do: Live well,*
> *live wisely, live humbly. It's the way you live, not*
> *the way you talk, that counts. Mean-spirited*
> *ambition isn't wisdom. Boasting that you are*
> *wise isn't wisdom. Twisting the truth to make*
> *yourselves sound wise isn't wisdom. It's the fur-*
> *thest thing from wisdom—it's animal cunning,*

devilish conniving. Whenever you're trying to look better than others or get the better of others, things fall apart and everyone ends up at the others' throats. Real wisdom, God's wisdom, begins with a holy life and is characterized by getting along with others. It is gentle and reasonable, overflowing with mercy and blessings, not hot one day and cold the next, not two-faced. You can develop a healthy, robust community that lives right with God and enjoy its results only if you do the hard work of getting along with each other, treating each other with dignity and honor (James 3:13-18 The Message).

The Bible also says:

We do, however, speak a message of wisdom among the mature, but not the wisdom of this age or of the rulers of this age, who are coming to nothing. No, we speak of God's secret wisdom, a wisdom that has been hidden and that God destined for our glory before time began. None of the rulers of this age understood it, for if they had, they would not have crucified the Lord of glory (1 Corinthians 2:6-7).

In the maze of the increase in knowledge of this age, as predicted in the Book of Daniel, intellectualism and rational deductions often override and even compulsively drive many human decisions. *"But you, O Daniel, shut up the words and seal the book, even to the time of the end: many shall run to and fro, and knowledge shall be increased"* (Dan. 12:4 KJV). The Bible says that the wisdom of this world will come to nothing. However, in a very subtle way, worldly wisdom tends to deceptively mimic and may be incredibly difficult to differentiate from the wisdom of God.

The wisdom of this world comes from satan and started in the Garden of Eden. When Eve, in disobedience to the commandment of God, saw that it (forbidden fruit) was *"desirable for gaining wisdom, she took some and ate it"* (Gen. 3:6). The desire to gain knowledge and become like God has continued to be the root of wisdom of this age to this day.

The Bible, however, says that, *"The fear of the Lord is the beginning of wisdom..."* (Prov. 9:10). It also says that, "the wisdom that comes from heaven is first of all pure, then peace-loving, considerate, submissive, full of mercy and good fruit, impartial and sincere" (James 3:17).

> The wisdom of this world comes from satan.

This godly wisdom needs to be sustained and guided in the experiential knowledge of God, because wisdom that is devoid of the knowledge of God is futile. Solomon was the wisest king who ever lived, but when he applied his own wisdom contrary to the knowledge of God, it became corrupted. He, therefore, slid into a life of sin and iniquity. Unguided strength will ultimately become a double weakness. That is why God admonishes us in Jeremiah:

> *Let not the wise man boast of his wisdom or the strong man boast of his strength or the rich man boast of his riches, but let him who boasts about this: that he understands and knows Me, that I am the Lord, who exercises kindness, justice and righteousness on earth, for in these I delight* (Jeremiah 9:23-24).

Characteristics of Wisdom from God

God is pure and only pure wisdom leads to peace. It does not matter how smart it seems, if it is devoid of peace, it is not of God. God's wisdom has no strife, is quick to listen, and slow to speak. It is willing to submit to others in Christ Jesus. It does not win the argument and lose a brother. It judges not, is ready to forgive, and never

> Unguided strength will ultimately become a double weakness.

takes revenge. It shows no favoritism nor does it take sides. It has absolutely no hypocrisy—actions match words. It speaks the truth in love—do not desire to bring someone down by openly speaking the truth; there is always a way to speak the truth that would be mutually beneficial.

As mentioned previously, wisdom has a beginning: *"The fear of the Lord is the beginning of wisdom"* (Prov. 9:10) and it is a choice you have to make. *"If any of you lacks wisdom, he should ask God"* (James 1:5). Wisdom is the main thing, that is why it is described as the principal thing in all our dealings, *"Wisdom is the supreme; therefore get wisdom. Though it cost all you have, get understanding"* (Prov. 4:7).

All forms of wisdom are transferable. *"Now Joshua son of Nun was filled with the spirit of wisdom because Moses had laid his hands on him…"* (Deut. 34:9). However, be careful who lays hands on you, because the spirit of folly is also transferable. Spiritual wisdom is corruptible. *"Your heart became proud on account of your beauty, and you corrupted your wisdom because of your splendor…"* (Ezek. 28:17).

Wisdom is an expendable commodity as well as being corruptible. Wisdom needs to be constantly renewed or sharpened; this is often the reason why some wise people can do foolish things. Wisdom, however, can also increase just as Jesus grew strong in spirit full of wisdom (see Luke 2:40). It is also given for a specific service. For instance, Bezalel was given a specific wisdom for the divine purpose of building the tabernacle for God:

> *Then Moses said to the Israelites, "See, the Lord has chosen Bezalel son of Uri, the son of Hur, of the tribe of Judah, and He has filled him with the Spirit of God, with skill, ability and knowledge in all kinds of crafts—to make artistic designs…* (Exodus 35:30-32).

Spiritual wisdom should not be used against the purpose of God, *"There is no wisdom, no insight, no plan that can succeed against the Lord"* (Prov. 21:30). Ahithophel was a great man of wisdom and a trusted counselor to David, but when he conspired against David, the anointed king of Israel, David prayed, *"O Lord, turn Ahithophel's counsel into foolishness"* (2 Sam. 15:31). His wise counsel was frustrated by God and rejected by Absalom, and he ended up committing suicide.

Practical Aspects of the Wisdom of God

In general, the wisdom of God is about the following:

- Becoming skillful in honoring our parents
- Raising children in a godly way
- Honoring marriage vows

- Handling money wisely
- Conducting sexual lives in a godly way
- Having the right attitude toward work or career

Wisdom also means exercising our physical bodies (the human body is the temple of God), learning the skills and values of godly leadership, and allowing God to curb our tongue, especially when we are under pressure (the Bible says that we will be judged by the words of our mouth). Wisdom of God means having the right relationship with other people, these are our horizontal relationships. Our relationship with God is our vertical relationship and is dependent to a great extent on our horizontal relationships. Through wisdom, we also come to the realization that eating and drinking healthily is essential as we are reaching for the top.

Factors that Can Corrupt Spiritual Wisdom

- Pride – As the Bible says, *"Your heart became proud on account of your beauty, and you corrupted your wisdom because of your splendor..."* (Ezek. 28:17).

- Lust and selfish ambition – Solomon *"had seven hundred wives of royal birth and three hundred concubines, and his wives led him astray"* (1 Kings 11:3). This is apostle James' conclusion, *"if you harbor bitter envy and selfish ambition in your hearts, do not boast about it or deny the truth. Such 'wisdom' does not come down from heaven but is earthly, unspiritual, of the devil"* (James 3:15).

- Bad company – Don't be deceived; bad company corrupts. Folly is a transferable spirit.

- Willful sins – David prayed, *"Keep your servant also from willful sins; may they not rule over me. Then will I be blameless, innocent of great transgression"* (Ps. 19:13). Willful sins gradually defile the mind and conscience, leading to insensitivity to the promptings of the Holy Spirit.

- Sentiment – Jonathan, son of Saul, was so sentimentally attached to his father that he could not influence the situation, even though Jonathan knew that the Spirit of God had left the house of Saul. Despite his good intentions, Jonathan died in the "wrong house," and all he left behind was a crippled son.

DESTINY DELIBERATIONS

1   "It is impossible to obtain spiritual wisdom and knowledge without knowing Christ—and Christ crucified."

Question: Why is this truth so important to understand?

_____

_____

2. "Wisdom needs to be constantly renewed and sharpened; this is often the reason why some wise people can do foolish things."

Question: Have you done foolish things because your spiritual wisdom is dull?

_____

_____

Question: Is reading God's Word regularly the best way to sharpen your spiritual wisdom?

_____

_____

3. "Wisdom of God means having the right relationship with other people...and with God."

   Question: On a scale of 1-10, how would you rate the majority of your relationships with other people?

   _____

   _____

   Question: With God?

   _____

   _____

Chapter 5

Living Righteously: Avoiding Sexual Sins

The Devil, Spirituality, and Sexuality

WHEN Israel posed a military threat to Moab, the Moabites, on the advice of Balaam, used the age-long vulnerability to sexual sin to subvert Israel spiritually.

> *While Israel was staying in Shittim, the men began to indulge in sexual immorality with Moabite women, who invited them to the sacrifices to their gods. The people ate and bowed down before these gods. So Israel joined in worshiping the Baal of Peor. And the Lord's anger burned against them* (Numbers 25:1-3).

Likewise in these modern times, the increase and fervency of the unfolding Christianity across the world is threatening the domain of the kingdom of darkness, and counter offensives from the devil are, therefore, to be expected.

Sexual desire is easily the most common idol in the hearts of men and women. Threats using sexual bait are an ancient strategy of the evil world. Time and time again, God allegorized the sin of idolatry with the sin of sexual promiscuity and immorality. In ancient times, pagan religious worship incorporated adultery into its rituals. Pagans believed that sexual rituals, through occult prostitution, would ecstatically put them in tune with supernatural powers. Somehow, in those times, the people recognized a connection between the intensity of sexual ecstasy and spirituality (operating in the supernatural).

These sexual rituals were common at pagan religious shrines, which were located at the high places or hilltops in biblical days. These prostitutes were referred to as "shrine prostitutes." Whenever this practice was entrenched in Israel, it perverted spirituality that became difficult to eradicate. Even the patriarch Judah fell victim to the service of a pretend shrine prostitute:

> *When Tamar was told, "Your father-in-law is on his way to Timnah to shear his sheep," she took off her widow's clothes, covered herself with*

a veil to disguise herself, and then sat down at the entrance to Enaim, which is on the road to Timnah. For she saw that, though Shelah had now grown up, she had not been given to him as his wife. When Judah saw her, he thought she was a [shrine] prostitute, for she had covered her face. Not realizing that she was his daughter-in-law, he went over to her by the roadside and said, "Come now, let me sleep with you." "And what will you give me to sleep with you?" she asked (Genesis 38:13-16).

Modern-day "shrine prostitution" is the reemergence and repackaging of the old tricks of the devil with modern flavor. Modern-day shrine prostitutes are those males or females who flaunt sexuality under the cover of apparent spiritual weakness. They appear spiritually naïve and needing help, but often their desire is far from being helped and instead want to lure victims into carnal desires. The truth is that the minds of these people are so defiled that they believe no one can overcome sexual temptation if the temptation is persistent and if the conditions are ripe. This is self-justification and forms the premise on which they are bold enough to tempt newcomers and even the head of the congregation!

This is different from the spirit of Jezebel. The Jezebel spirit is an extreme and wicked form of witchcraft, often operating from the place of strength and propelled by sexual exploitation. The Jezebel spirit targets primarily the prophet/seer anointing; whereas the spirit of modern-day shrine prostitution often aims mainly at the pastoral and evangelistic anointing—the high-profile preachers.

The shrine prostitutes most times appear to be vulnerable, naïve, and spiritually weak; but in reality, they have no genuine desire to grow in the things of God. They need to be helped, and this should entail removing the unbelief, training to renew thinking, and firmly instilling Christian values. This often takes a protracted process; but in dealing with this spirit, firmness and strict adherence to rules of principled leadership are required.

Satan's Strategy

The Moabite women offered sexual favors and then invited the Israelites to their idol worshiping. This strategy of satan continues even to this day, and is biting hard at us in an ever-increasing pattern. The fall of any anointed servant of God is not only a personal loss but also a loss to the generation to which the servant was sent. God anoints His servants for His specific purposes. As the Bible says, "*The Spirit of the Sovereign*

Lord is on me because the Lord has anointed me to preach good news to the poor. He has sent me to bind up the brokenhearted, to proclaim freedom for the captives and release from darkness for the prisoners" (Isa. 61:1).

One of the remits of this particular anointing, therefore, is to bring freedom to those who are bound. Every anointing has its specific purpose and service to the Body of Christ. Thus, the benefits are more to the other saints than to the carrier of the anointing. This is why some anointed people, despite falling in the sight of God, can continue to be used for a time to help other saints, because the Shepherd is interested in the welfare of His flock. After all, God can use a donkey!

Church Invasion

The spirit of modern-day shrine prostitution is invading church gatherings with unacceptable, extreme provocation of sexy social fashion. I believe Christians should be fashionable; after all, Jesus' garment was so valuable and fashionable that the soldiers cast lots to divide it. "They divided up His clothes by casting lots" (Luke 23:34b). But decency and common sense have boundaries beyond which it becomes excessive. The original designer of "cleavage" might have had good and decent intentions, but this fashion trend has transcended the borders of decency and now amounts to indecent and extremely embarrassing exposure of female breasts. Worse still, this style is invading the church with reckless abandon—and a majority of Christians are quiet about it. Eyesight is the major gateway for evil thoughts to get into people's minds and spirits, particularly men. Let's protect the anointing!

One of the greatest puzzles of our times is how a highly gifted, anointed servant of God can so easily become prey to the weak and crispy spirit that I refer to as modern-day shrine prostitution. The fact is that this spirit works by gradual, slow, and steady corruption of the spiritual wisdom that propels the giftedness. The subtlety is often difficult to detect. Once the servant dwells on the thought suggested directly or indirectly by this spirit, it becomes a desire over time. Desires crave for action if the thought is not aborted soon enough. The first action is hard and difficult, but the second time becomes routine, repetitious, and much easier. Repeat actions lead to habit, and habits are hard to break! Repeated evil actions are prone to further repetition and this leads to defilement of minds and conscience, *"but even their mind and conscience are defiled"* (Titus 1:15b NKJV). A defiled mind loses the ability to discern what is wholesome from what is unwholesome. Then the mighty can fall in the midst of the battle.

> The grip of sexual immorality leads to corrupt wisdom

Sexual Detours

Sexual bondage is peculiar. It creeps in subtly, but grips with so much intensity, overwhelming its victims with such a passion, that reason and logic are easily thrown into the abyss. This addiction can be traced to the image center of our inner selves. The image center is the pictorial depository of our imagination. The grip and enticement of pictures in our imagination is hard to suppress and the addiction difficult to overcome. Therefore, for those with revelatory giftedness, it becomes a snare because revelations are also translated to our image center for processing and understanding.

A sanctified imagination is important for receiving and handling revelations from God; for example, a person with a watchman's[1] anointing and a corrupted imagination emanating from sexual sin pollutes the image center making the watchman's reception blurred and distorted so that the prophets stumble at giving prophecy. Do not allow sexual sin or inordinate sexual indulgence to subvert your walk with God.

Let's look at the turning points in the lives of two great kings. Chapter 11 of the Book of Second Samuel was to King David what chapter 11 of First Kings was to King Solomon. For both kings, these chapters record events that constituted the turning points in their reigns as kings and entail the painful consequences of their sins. Their stories might have been different if they had avoided the detours that emanated from their sexual weaknesses and overindulgence.

For King David, this was his count:

> *In the spring, at the time when kings go off to war, David sent Joab out with the king's men and the whole Israelite army. They destroyed the Ammonites and besieged Rabbah. But David remained in Jerusalem. One evening David got up from his bed and walked around on the roof of the palace. From the roof he saw a woman bathing. The woman was very beautiful, and David sent someone to find out about her. The man said, "She is Bathsheba, the daughter of Eliam and the wife of Uriah the Hittite." Then David sent messengers to get her. She came to him, and he slept with her. (Now she was purifying herself from her monthly uncleanness.) Then she went back home. The woman conceived and sent word to David, saying, "I am pregnant"* (2 Samuel 11:1-5).

> *Then Nathan said to David, "You are the man! This is what the LORD, the God of Israel, says: 'I anointed you king over Israel, and I delivered*

you from the hand of Saul. I gave your master's house to you, and your master's wives into your arms. I gave you all Israel and Judah. And if all this had been too little, I would have given you even more. Why did you despise the word of the LORD by doing what is evil in his eyes? You struck down Uriah the Hittite with the sword and took his wife to be your own. You killed him with the sword of the Ammonites (2 Samuel 12:7-9).

For King Solomon, this was his count;

King Solomon, however, loved many foreign women besides Pharaoh's daughter—Moabites, Ammonites, Edomites, Sidonians and Hittites. They were from nations about which the LORD had told the Israelites, "You must not intermarry with them, because they will surely turn your hearts after their gods." Nevertheless, Solomon held fast to them in love. He had seven hundred wives of royal birth and three hundred concubines, and his wives led him astray. As Solomon grew old, his wives turned his heart after other gods, and his heart was not fully devoted to the

*LORD his God, as the heart of David his father
had been* (1 Kings 11:1-4).

After these events, the reigns of both kings detoured and
became fraught with pain, suffering, violence, conspiracy, and
rebellion.

The news of a modern-day minister falling victim to this
evil strategy sends shock waves around the world. Yet worse
still is the silent evil of pornography and the sexual laxity that
are quietly eating deeply into the cutting edge of anointed men
and women of God. More than ever before we need people
with an Epaphras spirit—those who will stand in the gap for
those in the frontline battle zones with cutting-edge anointing
to run their race to the finishing line as willed by God:

> *Epaphras who is one of yourselves, a servant of
> Christ Jesus, sends you greetings. [He is] always
> striving for you earnestly in his prayers, [plead-
> ing] that you may [as persons of ripe character
> and clear conviction] stand firm and mature [in
> spiritual growth], convinced and fully assured
> in everything willed by God* (Colossians 4:12
> AMP).

One of the offensive attacks of satan on the church is compromise in the Christian standards masquerading as tolerance.

Even Moses also had to deal with this spirit of compromise when it reared its head among the Israelites on their way to the Promised Land. Moses was infuriated, *"Have you allowed all the women to live?" he asked them. They were the ones who followed Balaam's advice and enticed the Israelites to be unfaithful to the Lord in the Peor incident, so that a plague struck the Lord's people"* (Num. 31:15-16).

Corrupted Wisdom

In general, corruption of the wisdom that propels any giftedness is perhaps more common than we often imagine. Wisdom that drives giftedness becomes corrupt when the original purity of the wisdom becomes perverted through the frailty or hubris of humanity. The danger of corrupt wisdom is the subtlety with which it creeps into the life of its victim. This is why the Bible says let people who think they stand take heed lest they fall (see 1 Cor. 10:12). The Bible says of satan, *"Your heart was lifted up* [with pride] *because of your beauty; you corrupted your wisdom for the sake of your splendor..."* (Ezek. 28:17 NKJV).

Corrupted wisdom is menacing us every day at an alarming rate. The difficulty is that often the miracles of healings, financial breakthroughs, raising the dead, or other supernatural signs make a spectacle of the sovereignty and supremacy of

God. That in itself is desirable, for it adds to the effectiveness of reaching out to the unsaved and those with whom God seeks to communicate. But these experiences are also the avenues by which satan lures many into excesses, self-exaltation, and sexual immorality.

King Solomon was described as the wisest king who ever lived; he *"was greater in riches and wisdom than all the other kings of the earth. All kings of the earth sought audience with Solomon to hear the wisdom God had put in his heart"* (2 Chron. 9:22-23). Nevertheless, Solomon slid in a very subtle way into disobedience, a cleverly maneuvered pattern that men cannot perceive. A passion or giftedness that is not properly harnessed will lead to perversion. Solomon's uncontrolled sexual exploits led to his descent into moral decadence with cleverly maneuvered subtlety.

> A passion or giftedness that is not properly harnessed will lead to perversion.

There are ways we can recognize satan's tactics before they overtake us. We can be victorious over sin.

Endnote

1.   *Watchman: the ministry of the seer in a local church.*

DESTINY DELIBERATIONS

1. "Modern-day shrine prostitutes are those males or females who flaunt sexuality under the cover of apparent spiritual weakness."

   Question: Do you know people who fit into this category?

   _____

   _____

   Question: Have you been affected by them in ways that caused you to sin?

   _____

   _____

2. "The grip and enticement of pictures in our imagination is hard to suppress and the addiction difficult to overcome."

   Question: How true do you believe this statement is based on your personal experiences?

   _____

   _____

   Question: How do you keep your imagination pure?

   _____

   _____

3. "A passion or giftedness that is not properly harnessed will lead to perversion."

Question: Has your passion or giftedness been perverted?

_____

_____

Question: If so, write down steps you can take to get back on track.

_____

_____

Chapter 6

Living Victoriously Over Sin

Let sin have no dominion over us.

Therefore also now, says the Lord, turn and keep on coming to Me with all your heart, with fasting, and weeping, and with mourning [until every hindrance is removed and the broken fellowship is restored] (Joel 2:12 AMP).

A S long as we live in these earthen vessels, sin will continue to be reproach to the fallen human race:

If we say that we have no sin, we deceive ourselves, and the truth is not in us (1 John 1:8 NKJV).

> *For all have sinned and fall short of the glory of God* (Romans 3:23).

God gave us all clear instructions about how to handle sin when He said to Cain, *"...sin is crouching at your door; it desires to have you, but you must master it"* (Gen. 4:7). The central issue, therefore, is not that sin will not crouch at your door, but that it should have no dominion over you, and that we must master the art of stopping sin when it is at the door. As the Bible says:

> *Direct my steps by Your word, and let no iniquity have dominion over me* (Psalm 119:133 NKJV).

The writer of Hebrews further said, *"...let us lay aside every weight and the sin which so easily ensnares us, and let us run with endurance the race that is set before us"* (Heb. 12:1 NKJV). Many people have attained greatness because they have gained mastery over their point of susceptibility to the sin that so easily besieged them. The phrase "to master" (see Gen. 4:7) implies a continuous reliance on God, who is able to stop us from falling and who allows us to

> People attain greatness because they gained mastery over the sin that so easily besieged them.

"approach the throne of grace with confidence, so that we may receive mercy and find grace to help us in our time of need" (Heb. 4:16).

Sin is the transgression of the law. An understanding of the dynamics of sin is essential to our daily walk with God. This is the way I understand this: God made the world and set down rules, which would keep things running peacefully and without pain and suffering. When these rules are maintained, peace, love, and harmony ensue. But when God's rules are broken, it is called sin and pain and suffering ensue. As descendants of Adam, we have all broken these rules, and therefore we are all sinners. Humankind acquired a sinful nature when Adam and Eve disobeyed God's commandment not to eat of the forbidden fruit. Even in this present age, the breaking of God's rules is the consequence of this acquired sinful nature— the root cause of all the problems in the world.

The Consequences of Sin and Christ's Redemption of Humankind

There are two sides to the consequences of sin—guilt and punishment. Guilt comes from being responsible for a wrongdoing, whereas punishment is the penalty for this wrongdoing. The Bible makes a clear distinction between the two when it says, *"The Lord will not leave the guilty unpunished"* (Nah. 1:3) and *"You were to Israel a forgiving God, though You punished their misdeeds"* (Ps. 99:8), that is to say God forgave the guilt (erased the stain of the sin), but somehow they had to pay for the penalty of the sin. I believe these passages make it clear that forgiveness does not mean that God will not punish for doing wrong. God forgave David, yet David suffered the penalty of his adulterous relationship with Bathsheba. Psalm 32:5 makes this even more specific and clear:

> *Then I acknowledged my sin to you and did not cover up my iniquity, I said "I will confess my transgressions to the Lord"—and you forgave the guilt of my sin.*

When God forgives sin, He erases the guilt of the sin. However, every sin carries some form of penalty in one way or the other. However, the psalmist wrote, *"He has not dealt with us according to our sins, nor punished us according to our iniquities"* (Ps. 103:10 NKJV). But God said, *"I am the Lord, who exercises kindness, justice and righteousness on the earth, for in these I delight"* (Jer. 9:24). Notice that justice is sandwiched between kindness and righteousness.

The solution was that God came to earth Himself, in the person of His Son, to take away the destructive and addictive power of sin. By dying on the cross, He paid the death penalty on our behalf. Those who accept the sacrifice of Jesus on the cross of Calvary are acquitted. This is the basis and wonder of Jesus' sacrifice on the cross to redeem humankind.

Godly Sorrow Leads to True Repentance

If we confess our sins, God is faithful and righteous to forgive us our sins and to cleanse us from all unrighteousness. However, confession must be followed with godly sorrow for true repentance to take place. *"Godly sorrow brings repentance that leads to salvation and leaves no regret, but worldly sorrow brings death"* (2 Cor. 7:10).

True repentance always asks one crucial question: *"What will thou have me do?"* In Acts 2, the people cried out, *"Brothers, what shall we do?"* Paul, trembling and astonished on the road to Damascus, cried out to God, *"Lord what wilt though have me do?"* The keepers of the prison, seeing the miraculous release of Paul and Silas, cried out, *"Sirs, what must I do to be saved?"*

Breaking the Power of Sin

Sin has a compelling force that attracts or pulls. It entices, grips the mind intensely, defiles the conscience, perverts perception, and corrupts the wisdom of the victim. It may start in a vague, inoffensive, and subtle way, but it gradually becomes a domineering obsession.

The power of sin can be broken by:

- **Applying the blood**. The greatest testimony of all is when the Son of God declared on the cross: "It is finished!" Through His blood and the cross alone, He has broken the power of sin, death, and hell. The blood of Jesus washes away every sin and overcomes its power. No power can stand the proclamation of the blood of Jesus.

- **Dealing with the pleasure of sin**. The love of God overthrows the power of sin; this is expressed in John 14:15 (NKJV), *"If you love Me,* [then you will] *keep My commandments."* You don't keep His commandments to show that you love God; rather, the love of God enables you to keep His commandments. The pleasure of sin for those living in Sodom and Gomorrah was so strong that they failed to notice when they were under a special surveillance mission from God:

The two angels arrived at Sodom in the evening, and Lot was sitting in the gateway of the city. When he saw them, he got up to meet them and bowed down with his face to the ground.

"My lords," he said, "please turn aside to your servant's house. You can wash your feet and spend the night and then go on your way early in the morning." "No," they answered, "we will spend the night in the square." But he insisted so strongly that they did go with him and entered his house. He prepared a meal for them, baking bread without yeast, and they ate. Before they had gone to bed, all the men from every part of the city of Sodom—both young and old—surrounded the house. They called to Lot, "Where are the men who came to you tonight? Bring them out to us so that we can have sex with them." Lot went outside to meet them and shut the door behind him and said, "No, my friends. Don't do this wicked thing. Look, I have two daughters who have never slept with a man. Let me bring them out to you, and you can do what you like with them. But don't do anything to these men, for they have come under the protection of my roof." "Get out of our way," they replied. "This fellow came here as a foreigner, and now he wants to play the judge! We'll treat you worse than them." They kept bringing pres-

sure on Lot and moved forward to break down
the door (Genesis 19:1-9).

- **Dealing with the lust of the flesh**. In order to
  enjoy the abundance of life in the Holy Spirit, you
  must do away with your pre-conversion lifestyle.
  Your flesh is your soul (mind, emotion, and will),
  which is not ruled by your spirit. Redemption is
  the process of bringing the "fallen" soul under
  the rule of the spirit again. It is an active process,
  and you have to make a deliberate effort to obey
  your spirit rather than your flesh. If you walk in
  the spirit, you will not obey the lust of the flesh.
  Remember, you cannot cast out flesh; you must
  crucify flesh. Uncontrolled lustfulness can become
  a disease:

  In the course of time, Amnon son of David fell in
  love with Tamar, the beautiful sister of Absalom
  son of David. Amnon became so obsessed with
  his sister Tamar that he made himself ill. She
  was a virgin, and it seemed impossible for him
  to do anything to her (2 Samuel 13:1-2).

If your sinful nature is not crucified, it will prevent you
from moving into the Holy of Holies. The writer of Hebrew

puts it this way: *"By this the Holy Spirit points out that the way into the [true Holy of] Holies is not yet thrown open as long as the former [the outer portion of the] tabernacle [self] remains a recognized institution and is still standing"* (Heb. 9:8 AMP).

- **Dealing with the lust of the eyes**. Job said, *"I made a covenant with my eyes not to look lustfully at a girl"* (Job 31:1). Never has the principle been more relevant than now when nearly every television commercial starts with a sensual appeal, which bears no relevance to the product being advertised. The idea behind this way of advertising is to captivate the audience through the eyes and gradually introduce the object during the brief period of captivity. King David became a victim during such a brief period of captivity:

  In the spring, at the time when kings go off to war, David sent Joab out with the king's men and the whole Israelite army. They destroyed the Ammonites and besieged Rabbah. But David remained in Jerusalem. One evening David got up from his bed and walked around on the roof of the palace. From the roof he saw a woman bathing. The woman was very beautiful, and David sent someone to find out about her. The

> *man said, "She is Bathsheba, the daughter of Eliam and the wife of Uriah the Hittite." Then David sent messengers to get her. She came to him, and he slept with her. (Now she was purifying herself from her monthly uncleanness.) Then she went back home. The woman conceived and sent word to David, saying, "I am pregnant* (2 Samuel 11:1-5).

You become what you behold. We should make a conscious effort to resist the lust of the eyes. It has a magnetic hold on the emotion where it tends to linger, even when the music has long ceased. The eyes are the major gateway for sin to enter into a person's life, and men in particular are more prone to yielding to the sin of pornography than women. The major gateway of sin for women is in hearing, so women are more vulnerable and sensitive to what they hear than men.

- **Dealing with evil desire**. *"Do not let sin reign in your mortal body so that you obey its evil desires"* (Rom. 6:12). Every desire starts as a thought. The best time to stop sin is when it is still crouching at your door in the form of a thought. Examine every thought and dismiss any that are ungodly.

This is the process by which we are transformed by the renewal of our minds. The battle is in the mind; if we dwell on a thought long enough, it becomes a desire craving for action. The devil is after our thought-life, as the way we think will become the way we behave. Thoughts are our seeds into the future and out of them come the issues of our lives; so we must guard our hearts with all diligence. Take captive every thought to make it obedient to Christ.

- **Dealing with willful sin**. The psalmist declares, *"Keep Your servant also from willful sins; may they not rule over me. Then I will be blameless, innocent of great transgression"* (Ps. 19:13). In willful sin you know that it is wrong, but you commit it anyway because of the pleasure of the sin, or for some other satisfaction. This is often a deliberate act and is usually meticulously planned; it is different from when the righteous may incidentally stumble. Willful sin is usually an act carried out contrary to the prompting of the Holy Spirit and because it is prone to reoccur, it gradually leads to a blunt sensitivity to the prompting of the Holy Spirit. Hebrews 10:26 says, *"If we deliberately keep on sinning after we have received the knowledge of the truth, no sacrifice for sins is left."*

- **Dealing with hidden sin**. Pray that the Lord will reveal the hidden sins in your life. Hidden sins are sinful acts that you do not know are wrong. *"Who* *can discern his lapses and errors? Clear me from hidden [and unconscious] faults"* (Ps. 19:12 AMP).

Hidden sins are usually closely associated with strongholds. A stronghold is either a false belief that has been held for such a long time that it appears to be true (negative stronghold), or a belief in the established truth that is so firmly held that it becomes a protective divine shield (positive stronghold). The Bible says, *"The weapons we fight with are not the weapons of the world"* (2 Cor. 10:4). On the contrary, they have divine power to demolish strongholds. We can demolish arguments and every pretension that sets itself up against the knowledge of God, and we can take captive every thought to make it obedient to Christ.

- **Knowing that the struggle with sin is a continuous process.** Paul said, *"When I want to do good, evil is right there with me. For in my inner being I delight in God's law; but I see another law at work in the members of my body, waging war against the law of my mind and making me a prisoner of the law of sin at work within my members"* (Rom. 7:21-23).

The struggle goes on every day, which is why the Bible admonishes us to "die to self" on a daily basis. Paul said, *"I die every day"* (1 Cor. 15:31). Each time a fleshy desire resurrects, you should quickly put it to death again.

- **Learning the act of confession**. Confession is the acknowledgment, recognition, and acceptance of responsibility for a sinful act, and then admittedly bringing it to God knowing that it does not fit with who you are as a child of God. *"If we confess our sins, He is faithful and just and will forgive us our sins and purify us from all unrighteousness"* (1 John 1:9).

In confession, you should be specific; first in confessing to God, and second to prayerfully consider asking others for forgiveness. Public confession can only be done if it does not bring further hurt to anybody. Finally, keep turning to God until every hindrance is removed and the broken relationship restored.

Repentance

The power of sin can also be broken by repentance. To repent means to regret something that has been done and to change from this evil way. In the Hebrew language, repent literally means to turn around 180 degrees and move toward God. In the Greek language, it connotes a change of mind or a way of thinking. Both are applicable.

Repentance, therefore, represents a change of mind resulting from a well-motivated inner determination (will) that is deep-seated—not a temporary thing or short-lived experience. It should not be based just on an emotion, because emotion so quickly runs out. Inner conviction and motivation are essential.

- **Repentance leads to a life of faith in Christ**. *"Therefore, O house of Israel, I will judge you, each one according to his ways, declares the Sovereign LORD. Repent! Turn away from all your offenses; then sin will not be your downfall. Rid yourselves of all the offenses you have committed, and get a new heart and a new spirit. Why will you die, O house of Israel? For I take no pleasure in the death of anyone, declares the Sovereign LORD. Repent and live!"* (Ezek. 18:30-32)

The problem is that most people often mistake being remorseful as being repentant. Such people have not really repented but are only remorseful; and this happens about 50 percent of the time. Remorse is false repentance, because it does not emanate from a will borne out of a well-motivated decision, and it lacks a complete turn around that leads to God. Remember Judas? He was remorseful, but never really repented:

> *When Judas, who had betrayed him* [Christ], *saw that Jesus was condemned, he was seized*

with remorse and returned the thirty silver coins to the chief priest and elders. "I have sinned," he said, "for I have betrayed innocent blood" (Matthew 27:3-4).

On the other hand, Peter disowned Jesus three times, but he repented. As we read in Matthew 26:75, *"Then Peter remembered the word Jesus had spoken: 'Before the cock crows, you will disown Me three times.' And he went outside and wept bitterly."*

Remember also the prodigal son. He repented and went back to his father:

There was a man who had two sons. The younger one said to his father, "Father, give me my share of the estate." So he divided his property between them. Not long after that, the younger son got together all he had, set off for a distant country and there squandered his wealth in wild living. After he had spent everything, there was a severe famine of that country, who sent him to his fields to feed pigs. He longed to fill his stomach with the pods that the pigs were eating, but no one gave him anything.

When he came to his senses, he said, "How many of my father's hired men have food to spare, and here I am starving to death! I will set out and go back to my father and say to him: Father, I have sinned against heaven and against you. I am no longer worthy to be called your son; make me like one of your hired men." So he got up and went to his father. But while he was still a long way off, his father saw him and was filled with compassion for him; he ran to his son, threw his arms around him and kissed him.

The son said to him, "Father, I have sinned against heaven and against you. I am no longer worth to be called your son." But the father said to his servants, "Quick! Bring the best robe and put it on him. Put a ring on his finger and sandals on his feet. Bring the fattened calf and kill it. Let's have a feast to celebrate. For this son of mine was dead and is alive again; he was lost and is found." So they began to celebrate (Luke 15:11-24).

The process leading to true repentance involves one or many of the following:

- **Conviction of sins by the Spirit of God**. This is key to the process of repentance because the only true change comes from the Spirit:
  - Salvation comes from God
  - Coming to the end of self-reliance by default
  - Growing into the deeper things of God
  - Coming to the point of renewed desire to submit totally to God
  - Realizing that the house of God is the house of abundance
  - Realizing that all flesh will fail, which makes each one of us lean on God and find in Him what we could not find in anyone else
- **Hindrance to true repentance**. The devil has various means to keep people blind to the truth of God. These include:
  - Keeping them in ignorance
  - Making them feel worthless or proud
  - Making them dwell and place undue reliance on the opinion of the world around them
  - Keeping them from admitting failure and taking responsibility for the failure

- Making them feel that God will not accept and forgive them

Therefore let us leave elementary teachings about Christ and go on to maturity, not laying again the foundation of repentance from acts that lead to death, and of faith in God, instruction about baptisms, the laying on of hands, the resurrection of the dead, and eternal judgment (Hebrews 6:1-2).

This passage from Hebrews refers to the doctrinal foundations of our faith, which are:

- Repentance from dead works
- Faith in God
- Baptismal instructions
- The laying on of hands
- The resurrection of the dead
- Eternal judgment
- **How God responds to true repentance**. The story of the prodigal son illustrates that God is happy to forgive, accept, restore, and rejoice over the return of any and all sinners.

- **Repentance, faith, and the future**. Spiritual gifts of faith come only after genuine repentance. The spiritual gift of faith is the ability to see with the eyes of our hearts and beyond the limits of natural senses. John the Baptist preached repentance for the forgiveness of sins and also faith that the Messiah would come:

  He went into all the country around the Jordan, preaching a baptism of repentance for the forgiveness of sins. As is written in the book of Isaiah the prophet: A voice of one calling in the desert, "Prepare the way for the Lord, make straight paths for Him. Every valley shall be filled in, every mountain and hill made low. The crooked roads shall become straight, the rough ways smooth. And all mankind will see God's salvation" (Luke 3:3-6).

Jesus Christ preached further repentance and belief in the Good News, that the Kingdom of God is at hand: *"The time has come,"* He said. *"The kingdom of God is near. Repent and believe the good news!"* (Mark 1:15).

It is by faith that a person becomes born again. Faith is based and measured in terms of the things to come—spiritually.

DESTINY DELIBERATIONS

1. "Many people have attained greatness because they have gained mastery over their point of susceptibility to the sin that so easily besieged them."

   Question: Greatness can mean many things—do you believe that you will be great once you have mastered the sins in your life?

   _____

   _____

   Question: It is true. Believe it. How will your greatness affect your life? The people around you?

   _____

   _____

2. "Remember Judas? He was remorseful, but never really repented."

    Question: What is the difference between remorse and regret?

    _____

    _____

    Question: Write what you believe about both.

    _____

    _____

3. "The spiritual gift of faith is the ability to see with the eyes of our hearts and beyond the limits of natural senses."

   Question: What does this statement mean to you?

   _____

   _____

   Question: Do you take time to stop and see a situation, problem, or relationship with your heart's eyes?

   _____

   _____

Chapter 7

Living Spiritually with Simplicity of Heart

Let the little children come to Me, and do not hinder them, for the kingdom of heaven belongs to such as these (Matthew 19:14).

A life surrendered to God is a life of simplicity of heart (spiritual simplicity). God is delighted to see us come to a place of absolute spiritual simplicity, innocence, and dependency on Him, but this may be hard to attain in these days when times are perilous. Nevertheless, living spiritually was epitomized by the life that Adam and Eve lived in the Garden of Eden. Man's stay in the Garden of Eden was the age of innocence and a state of near spiritual purity. God's original intention was for His children to enjoy a state of childlike spirituality and honesty. Many of those who are experiencing the joy of dependency on God today are those who have understood how we must come to God as little children—come to our heavenly Father with confidence and boldness in transparent innocence.

Our goal must be to regain and retain this state of spiritual simplicity that existed in the Garden of Eden despite the evils of the day. It does not matter what is happening each day as each day has something to teach us, so we should continue in the confidence of who God is, even on our worst day. The power of God in us is entrenched in our realization of the fatherhood of God and in a life of total abandonment to His sovereignty.

The Lord Jesus Christ emphasized the divine premium on childlike attributes saying, *"I tell you the truth, unless you change and become like little children, you will never enter the kingdom of heaven. Therefore, whoever humbles himself like this little child is the greatest in the kingdom of heaven"* (Matt. 18:3-4).

The path to great things in God is the way of simplicity of heart and humility.

Worldly Complexities Versus Spiritual Simplicity

No wonder, therefore, that there is a connection between possessing a childlike simplicity and tapping into the nature of God when dealing with the pressures and doubts that may come across the seasons of our lives. I am persuaded that a state of spiritual simplicity must have prevailed in the Garden of Eden, prior to the fall of man, in order to have allowed the level of intimacy that Adam and Eve enjoyed with God. Unfortunately, when man chose to eat of the forbidden fruit, their natural eyes were opened. Man became self-conscious and acquired the knowledge of good and bad through the work of the activated soul. The activated soul slid out of the rule of the spirit and became separated from God, and this soul is called "flesh" or carnality.

This activated soul has a natural tendency to acquire earthly wisdom and human knowledge. Even to this day humankind is driven by the activated soul to expand its knowledge in a world that's regulated by the value outside the perimeters of God-ordained statutes. Flesh and the resulting increase in knowledge have continued to plague humanity ever since. Daniel alluded to the maze that has followed the increase in human knowledge when he said, *"Many shall run to and fro, and knowledge shall increase,"* in the end times (see Dan. 12:4 NKJV).

Thanks to God from whom all blessings flow that He has not repaid us with punishment that our sins deserve. Instead, He has, in His infinite mercy, put in place the process of redeeming humankind to Himself. Salvation is a process of bringing the activated soul under the rule of the spirit once again. It is a continuous process, so we are saved and are being saved.

The times the mind, emotion, and the human will predominate, are the times when we are operating from within the soul realm, making it hard to discern spiritual things. God loves spiritual simplicity; this is why the Bible says, *"Out of the mouths of babies and nursing infants You* [God] *have ordained strength…that you may silence the enemy and the avenger"* (Ps. 8:2 NKJV).

Pride Versus Spiritual Simplicity

The opposite of spiritual simplicity is the spirit of the world. I refer to this as the spirit of Uzziah because it is typified by the spirit that drove King Uzziah to pride. This spirit has a reliance on the works of worldliness and achievements of man.

God helped Uzziah to develop earthly systems to sustain his agricultural, political, and military prowess, *"As long as he* [Uzziah] *sought the Lord, God gave him success"* (2 Chron. 26:5).

> *Uzziah built towers in Jerusalem at the corner gate, at the valley Gate and at the angle of the wall, and he fortified them. He also built towers*

*in the desert and dug many cisterns, because
he had much livestock in the foothills and in
the plain. He had people working his fields and
vineyards in the hills and in the fertile lands,
for he loved the soil. Uzziah had a well-trained
army ready to go out by divisions…* (2 Chronicles 26:9-11).

In modern terms, Uzziah had it all worked out. However, there is always a hidden danger in having such a mentality.

In his pride, Uzziah abandoned God and relied on earthly achievements to sustain him. In those days, people believed in the systems that Uzziah had put in place instead of believing in the Lord who had given him the wisdom for the achievements. Even God's elects of those days were not exempted from such a mentality. The prophet Isaiah said, *"In the year that King Uzziah died, I saw the Lord seated on the throne, high and exalted, and the train of His robe filled the temple"* (Isa. 6:1). By inference, there were things that hindered a great prophet like Isaiah from seeing the only true God in His full majesty during the lifetime of King Uzziah.

If we want to see the Lord high and exalted in our days, we must take our eyes

> In the coming months and years, God will shake the systems that are currently in place.

off the world systems. In the coming months and years, God will shake the systems that are currently in place, which perpetuate the spirit of Uzziah, so that the eyes of those with Isaiah's gifting will be lifted up to see the Lord in His glory and majesty.

For us to return to the power of child-like simplicity, we must first deal with the spirit of Uzziah. This spirit thrives on earthly knowledge, man-made securities, and a reliance on worldly systems. Yet, we are not of this world, and our focus should be on the things above, all of the time. Power abounds in unadulterated and simple innocence, and we ought to return to this state of spiritual naivety—into the hands of our Almighty God. When we do this, we will regain what the devil has taken from us.

> Power abounds in unadulterated and simple innocence.

This is how God blessed us in our state of innocence: *"Be fruitful and increase in number, fill the earth and subdue it. Rule over the fish of the sea and the birds of the air and every living creature that moves on the ground"* (Gen. 1:28). This is the origin of divine impartation of the ability for easy increase.

It must be said that the only true Source of power is God. Indeed, the Bible says, *"power belongs to God"* (Ps. 62:11b) and *"It is not by strength that one prevails"* (1 Sam. 2:9).

Consequently, true blessing comes from the only true Source of power; all good and perfect gifts come from God, in whom there is no variableness or shadow of doubt (see James 1:17). On our part, we must approach Him with spiritual simplicity.

Spiritual Simplicity and Walking in Humility

Spiritual simplicity is a prerequisite to walking in humility. God resists the proud but gives grace to the humble. Therefore, let's humble ourselves in the hands of our God. Humility and pride are opposite poles in God's measurement. Pride is a sin against God Himself, against His very being, and against His sovereignty. It is like a fist to His face. It is also defilement to the nature of God and draws us away from Him. God will not use a prideful vessel, because He resists the proud and He will not share His glory with any other. Pride is a camouflaged usurpation of the glory that belongs to God.

Pride is a sin that originates from human strength. It is the most dangerous of all sins, because it is cunning and deceptive in its methods and speaks of reliance on human strength. Zephaniah—writing after the brutal reign of the worst king in the history of Judah, Manasseh, and at a time as perilous as the one we live in now—wrote

> Pride is a sin that originates from human strength.

of hope for the faithful and humble remnants who would be sheltered by God if they sought the Lord: *"Seek the Lord, all you humble of the land, you who do what He commands. Seek righteousness, seek humility; perhaps you will be sheltered on the day of the Lord's anger"* (Zeph. 2:3).

> *On that day you will not be put to shame for all the wrongs you have done to Me, because I will remove from this city those who rejoice in their pride. Never again will you be haughty on My holy hill. But I will leave within you the meek and humble, who trust in the name of the Lord* (Zephaniah 3:11-12).

Also when speaking on the same subject, Jesus said, *"Blessed are the meek, for they will inherit the earth"* (Matt. 5:5).

Our legacy to the future generations must be in our testimony that reflects nothing more than the evidence of our total reliance on God. Like Samuel, let us be bold to say, *"Thus far has the Lord helped us"* (1 Sam. 7:12). We must be bold to tell our future generations that, *"Because of the Lord's great love we are not consumed, for His compassions never fail. They are new every morning; great is Your faithfulness"* (Lam. 3:22-23).

God also said in Isaiah 2:17, *"The arrogance of man will be brought low and the pride of men humbled; the Lord alone will be exalted in that day."* Simplicity and humility entail learning how to give honor to God and how not to draw undue attention to ourselves.

Spiritual Simplicity and the
Angels of Innocence

Simplicity in the spirit is conjoined with the inclination to dependency on God and also with the activation of our guardian angels. Each one of us has more than one guardian angel: *"For He will command His angels concerning you to guard you in all your ways; they will lift you up in their hands, so that you will not strike your foot against a stone"* (Ps. 91:11-12).

God also released a corporate guardian angel on behalf of the Israelites:

> *See, I am sending an angel ahead of you to guard you along the way and to bring you to the place I have prepared. Pay attention to him and listen to what he says. Do not rebel against him; he will not forgive your rebellion, since My Name is in him* (Exodus 23:20-21).

Jesus also mentioned another guardian angel:

> *See that you do not look down on one of these little ones. For I tell you that their angels in*

heaven always see the face of my Father in heaven (Matthew 18:10).

The "little ones" refers to the spiritually naïve or young Christians. The more we surrender to God and live the life of simplicity, the more these angels are activated on our behalf. These angels are involved with those who are innocent and cover the backs of such righteous people.

Testimony and History

Testimony is telling other people about the aspects of God's attributes, which have been revealed to us by the events and circumstances that we experience. History, on the other hand, is the story of what God has done for us. There is a thin line of difference between testimony and history, but both are important. Testimony always gives glory to God, but history, as a stand-alone, carries the risk of drawing attention to people and could inadvertently amount to sharing glory with God. Recalling history should always, therefore, be preceded by testimony. A beautiful example of this correct sequence of testimony followed by history is given by Daniel:

> *During the night the mystery was revealed to Daniel in a vision. Then Daniel praised the God of heaven and said, "Praise be to the name of*

God for ever and ever; wisdom and power are His. He changes times and seasons; He sets up kings and deposes them. He gives wisdom to the wise and knowledge to the discerning. He reveals deep and hidden things; He knows what lies in darkness; and light dwells with Him. I thank and praise You, O God of my fathers: You have given me wisdom and power; You have made known to me what we asked of You, and You have made known to us the dream of the king" (Daniel 2:19-23).

Notice that Daniel first of all highlighted the nature of God that was revealed to him, *"He reveals deep and hidden things"*— this is testimony. Then Daniel mentioned what God has specifically done for him on that occasion, *"made known to me what we asked"*—that is history!

Daniel was also known for his reverent and consistent prayer life—one that spared his life, and can do the same for you.

DESTINY DELIBERATIONS

1. "God's original intention was for His children to enjoy a state of childlike spirituality and honesty."

   Question: How far have we come from this original state God intended?

   _____

   _____

   Question: What is the worst aspect of this current state we're in?

   _____

   _____

2. "True blessing comes from the only true Source of power; all good and perfect gifts come from God."

    Question: What is one of the most good and perfect gifts that God gave you?

    _____

    _____

    Question: Have you thanked Him for it lately?

    _____

    _____

3. "Testimony is telling others about God's attributes that have been revealed to us by the events and circumstances that we experience."

   Question: When is the last time you shared God's attributes with someone?

   _____

   _____

   Question: What recent God-event have you told someone about?

   _____

   _____

Chapter 8

Living a Life of Prayer

The prayer of a righteous man is powerful and effective (James 5:16).

PRAYER is always addressed to God. It is the highest spiritual exercise that you can undertake, and it really changes things. It is also an exercise of faith. God hears prayers, but answers faith. Prayer puts you in touch with God and is the covenant exchange of human frailty for God's infinite power. Prayer is the act of humbling yourself in the hands of the Almighty God so that He can exalt you. Your ministry is only as effective as your prayer life is deep—and no person is greater than his or her prayer life. In the Book of James, we are told that the effective and fervent prayer of the righteous brings much reward and benefit.

Prayer is the act of communicating and communing with God. It represents the melting point of self-reliance, self-sufficiency, human autonomy, and the submission to the Supreme Authority and the provision of divinity. It is the avenue for exchanging our powerlessness for the power of the mighty God.

The worldly person thrives on the principle, "If it feels good, do it," and the ultimate objective in the world system is the achievement of self-reliance and self-sufficiency.

> God hears prayers, but answers faith.

Christians, on the other hand, know that, *"The steps of a good man are ordered by the Lord"* (Ps. 37:23 NKJV), that *"Men always ought to pray"* (Luke 18:1 NKJV), and to *"pray without ceasing"* (1 Thess. 5:17 NKJV). This is because we also know that *"the effective, fervent prayer of a righteous man avails much"* (James 5:16).

As we live in a world tending toward absolute humanism, we see a conflict at play. The principles that operate in the worldly pursuit run contrary to the basic fundamentals of Christian living. As it is said:

> *For the sinful nature desires what is contrary to the Spirit, and the Spirit what is contrary to the sinful nature. They are in conflict with each other, so that you do not do what you want* (Galatians 5:17).

Jesus said, *"Flesh gives birth to flesh, but the Spirit gives birth to spirit"* (John 3:6). Furthermore, *"Do you not know that friendship with the world is enmity with God? Whoever therefore wants to be a friend of the world makes himself an enemy of God"* (James 4:4 NKJV).

For those with misplaced zeal for worldly success, prayer is therefore an "indictment" on independent living, an embarrassing encroachment on the busy schedule. Unfortunately, many people consider themselves far too busy to pray, but the decision to pray should be predicated on the choices presented in Deuteronomy 30:19, *"...I have set before you life and death, blessings and curses. Now choose life, so that you and your children may live."*

The unfolding events around the world today have come with such great uncertainty and ecological and human destruction, that sooner or later everyone will see the need to fall on the knees in total surrender to God in a simple act of submission and desire for God's intervention—as the only One who can make the seemly impossible possible. With God nothing is impossible (see Luke 1:37). To tap into the infinite supremacy and sovereignty of God, we must bring our situation before Him who alone is able to stop us from falling. As the prophet Isaiah admonished us, *"Review the past for me, let us argue the matter together; state the case for your innocence"* (Isa. 43:26).

Steps to Receiving Prayer Answers

1. Cleanse your heart and mind.

The psalmist put this subject in its correct perspective when he said, *"If I regard iniquity in my heart, the Lord will not hear. But certainly God has heard me; He has attended to the voice of my prayer"* (Ps. 66:18-19 NKJV). In the Book of Proverbs, Solomon said, *"Above all else, guard your heart, for it is the wellspring of life"* (Prov. 4:23), and when speaking on the same subject, Jesus said that, *"Nothing enters man from outside which can defile him; but the things which come out of him..."* (Mark 7:15 NKJV).

Our God is a good God, and His hands are not too short nor His ears deaf. It is our iniquities that separate us from Him (see Isa. 59:2). Jesus said in Mark 11:25, *"And when you stand praying, if you hold anything against anyone, forgive him, so that your Father in heaven may forgive you yours sins."* Therefore, confess your sins before you pray and God, being faithful and just, will forgive.

2. Have confidence in God.

The righteous shall live by faith (see Gal. 3:11; Rom. 1:17). Jesus told His disciples, *"I tell you truth, if you have faith as small as a mustard seed, you can say to this mountain, 'Move from here to there' and it will move. Nothing will be impossible for you"* (Matt. 17:20). James said, *"Let him ask in faith, with no doubting"* (James 1:6 NKJV). And in First John we read, *"This is the confidence we have in approaching God: that if we ask anything according to His will, He hears us. And if we know that He hears us—whatever we ask—we know that we have what we asked of Him"* (1 John 5:14-15).

We are often hindered by a lack of confidence in God on specific issues even though we are somehow confident that He is able on other matters. This is why, in the story of two blind men, Jesus asked them a very specific question before He healed them: *"Do you believe I am able to do this? 'Yes, Lord,' they replied. Then He touched their eyes and said, 'According to your faith will it be done to you'; and their sight was restored. Jesus warned them sternly. 'See that no one knows about this'"* (Matt. 9:28-30).

3. Do not pray amiss.

Pray with the right motives, *"When you ask, you do not receive, because you ask with wrong motives, that you may spend what you get on your pleasures"* (James 4:3). You should seek first God's Kingdom and His righteousness, and all the things you need shall be given to you as well (see Matt. 6:33). Solomon asked for wisdom, and many other things were added to his request (see 1 Kings 3:5-14).

Also, in the prayers of Elijah on Mount Carmel, we read of a well-motivated prayer and the prompt response of God: *"'O Lord, God of Abraham, Isaac and Israel, let it be known today that You are God in Israel and that I am Your servant and have done all these things at Your command. Answer me, O Lord, answer me, so these people will know that You, O Lord, are God, and that You are turning their hearts back again.' Then the fire of the Lord fell and burned up the sacrifice, the wood, the stones and the soil, and also licked up the water in the trench"* (1 Kings 18:36-38).

Note that the motive behind this request was for a show of power over the gods of Baal, so that the hearts of the people would be turned back to God.

4. Pray with thanksgiving.

Even God was thankful and contented with each day's achievement when He created the world one day at a time. At the end of each day, He appreciated the work that was done: *"God saw it was good"* (see Gen. 1). *"Be joyful always; pray continually; give thanks in all circumstances, for this is God's will for you in Christ Jesus"* (1 Thess. 5:16-18). *"Do not be anxious for anything, but in everything, by prayer and petition, with thanksgiving, present your requests to God"* (Phil. 4:6).

5. Pray for one another.

There is a time to call on others to pray with you; James said, *"Is any one of you sick? He should call the elders of the church to pray over him and anoint him with oil in the name of the Lord. And the prayer offered in faith will make the sick person well; the Lord will raise him up. If he has sinned, he will be forgiven. Therefore confess your sins to each other and pray for each other so that you may be healed. The prayer of a righteous man is powerful and effective"* (James 5:14-16).

God inhabits the praises of His people. He has said that when two or more are gathered together in His name, He will be in their midst. So, *"Speak to one another with psalms, hymns, and spiritual songs."* And *"Submit to one another out of reverence for Christ"* (Eph. 5:19,21). We should also, *"Bear with each other and forgive whatever grievances you may have against one another. Forgive as the Lord forgave you"* (Col. 3:13).

6. Be humble.

In humility, pray for God's mercy, for *"It does not...depend on man's desire or effort, but on God's mercy"* (Rom. 9:16). *"God resists the proud, but gives grace to the humble"* (James 4:6 NKJV). Do you remember King Hezekiah? When he was ill and at the point of death, the prophet Isaiah told him that he was going to die. But Hezekiah *"turned his face to the wall and prayed to the Lord.*" He then wept bitterly and the Lord said, "*the God of your father David says I have heard your prayer and seen your tears; I will heal you*" (see 2 Kings 20:1-5). If we humble ourselves, He will hear our prayers.

7. Ask, and be specific.

Ask, and it will be given to you; seek, and you will find; knock, and it shall be opened for you (see Matt. 7:7). Speak your desire into existence. The power of life and death is in your tongue. The Bible says, "*...just as you have spoken in My hearing, so I will do to you*" (Num. 14:28 NKJV).

Jesus said to the two blind men "*...What do you want me to do for you?*" and they replied, "*We want our sight*" (Matt. 20:31-33). Spiritually, the fact that we have needs does not automatically constitute or translate into a request. So be sure you make your specific need known to God.

8. Base your prayers on the Word of God.

God says that His words will not return to Him void. Use the relevant Scriptures to bring your requests to God and plead your case. Jesus said, "*It is written: 'Man does not live on bread alone, but on every word that comes from the mouth of God'*" (Matt. 4:4). The Word of God says, "*...whatever you bind on earth will be bound in heaven...*" (Matt. 16:19).

9. Pray to the Father.

Jesus taught His disciples; *"In this manner, therefore pray: Our Father in heaven, hallowed be your name"* (Matt. 6:9). Pray and ask the Father in the name of Jesus Christ, *"I tell you the truth, anyone who has faith in Me will do what I have been doing. He will do even greater things than these, because I am going to the Father. And I will do whatever you ask in My name, so that the Son may bring glory to the Father"* (John 14:12-13).

10. Pray in the Spirit.

Our spirits bear witness with the Spirit of God, so when we pray in the spirit, we are not only built up inwardly, but we cover areas not known to our mind and reasoning; and the devil is unable to understand what we are saying. *"In the same way, the Spirit helps us in our weakness. We do not know what we ought to pray for, but the Spirit Himself intercedes for us with groans that words cannot express. And He who searches our hearts knows the mind of the Spirit, because the Spirit intercedes for the saints in accordance with God's will"* (Rom. 8:26-27). *"For anyone who speaks in a tongue does not speak to men but to God. Indeed, no one understands him; he utters mysteries with his spirit"* (1 Cor. 14:2).

11. Fear God and keep His Commandments.

Fearing God and keeping His commandments are the essence of humankind, just as the Bible reminds us, *"Now all has been heard; here is the conclusion of the matter: Fear God and keep His commandments, for this is the whole duty of man"* (Eccl. 12:13). Obeying God's commandments brings blessings and speedy answers to our prayers.

Intercessory Prayers

Intercessory prayer is the art of standing in the gap in prayer for other people. Every Christian should be an intercessor, but not everyone carries the same amount of burden to pray for others. Jesus Christ is the supreme example for all Christians, *"Therefore He is able to save completely those who come to God through Him, because He always lives to intercede for them"* (Heb. 7:25). *"For there is one God and one mediator between God and men, the man, Christ Jesus, who gave Himself as a ransom for all men—the testimony given in its proper time"* (1 Tim. 2:5-6).

I believe as Christ continues to make intercession for us as Christians we are in turn to intercede for the lost world, *"I urge, then, first of all, that requests, prayers, intercession and thanksgiving be made for everyone—for kings and all those in authority, that we may live peaceful and quiet lives in all godliness and holiness"* (1 Tim. 2:1-2).

Here are some ingredients for successful intercessory prayer:

- Agape love
- Good knowledge of the Word of God
- Consistent zeal for the things of God
- Spiritual fervency
- Sensitivity to the needs of others
- Availability for God's purpose
- Advocacy—willing to plead for others
- Ability to share the pains of others
- Obedience to God
- Accountability to those ahead of us and responsible to those below us

You are destined for the top. God gave you the ability and gifts to reach your God-given potential. These first eight chapters laid the groundwork for you to jump face-forward into a future filled with hope and confidence.

The next part of the book, Family Issues, focuses on the realm of individual relationships and gives you the principles to apply to your life so you can be the best person possible, have the most mutually satisfying marriage possible, and become the Christian who pleases God.

DESTINY DELIBERATIONS

1. "Prayer puts you in touch with God and is the covenant exchange of human frailty for God's infinite power. Prayer is the act of humbling yourself in the hands of the Almighty God so that He can exalt you."

   Question: Have you ever considered this statement regarding prayer?

   _____

   _____

   Question: First, you humble yourself, then you are exalted. Explain this in your own words.

   _____

   _____

2. "We are often hindered by a lack of confidence in God on specific issues even though we are somehow confident that He is able on other matters."

   Question: Do you have a lack of confidence in God for some things and not other things?

   _____

   _____

   Question: Why?

   _____

   _____

3. "You are destined for the top. God gave you the ability and gifts to reach your God-given potential."

    Question: Do you believe you will reach the top with God's help?

    _____

    _____

    Question: Have you identified your God-given abilities and gifts?

    _____

    _____

PART II
FAMILY ISSUES

Chapter 9

Marriage

A Union in Flesh and in Spirit

G OD created male and female in His image, according to His likeness (see Gen. 1:26). Though both Adam and Eve had individual identities and possessed reflections of the attributes of God, it was their union as a husband and wife that gave them the privilege of beginning the human race and expressing the full likeness of the nature of God on earth; their ability to procreate, *"Has not the Lord made them one? In flesh and spirit they are His. And why one? Because He seeks godly offspring. So guard yourself in your spirit, and do not break faith with the wife of your youth"* (Mal. 2:15). The husband and wife are meant to be one, not only in flesh but also in spirit to ensure godly offspring.

A Covenant Union

The Lord God said, "It is not good for the man to be alone. I will make him a helper suitable for him." For this reason a man will leave his father and mother and be united to his wife, and they will become one flesh (Genesis 2:18,24).

Flesh is more than the body; it includes the soul. The man and the woman should be one in mind, emotion, and will. Union in these four areas—body, emotion, will, and mind—is pivotal to the success of the marriage. In Malachi 2:15, God added another dimension to the union in flesh that is oneness in the spirit. This means togetherness in communing with God, togetherness in studying and growing in the Word of God, and togetherness in learning to put the interests of other people first, preferring the interest of others to personal agenda. These are the practical dynamics of the sanctified conscience in operation.

A covenant is principally made when there are differences. It can create strength, security, and harmony in such diversity. A marriage, therefore, explores the differences between the man and the woman for the common good.

When two people are married, they bring memories of their experiences into the marriage, which shape the way in which they understand the world, their partner, and the marriage. It takes time, honesty, patience, commitment, and tolerance to overcome these differences. Success in marriage also depends, among other things, on the manliness of the husband, the meekness of the woman, and the guidance from God.

> Every marriage starts bilingual with the language of the man and the language of the woman.

Every marriage also starts as bilingual with the language of the man and the language of the woman. Usually it has no interpreter. Each has to learn the language of the other, bridging many language barriers—body language, spoken language, emotional language, spiritual language, and the language of experience—will lead to greater understanding in the marriage.

The marriage covenant is unique because the Lord commands two to become one flesh. It is also solemn and binding for life. Marriage has God as its third strand and is the basic fabric of existence and procreation of the human race. When God deals with man it is and always has been with a covenant basis: marriage is a covenant relationship with a high divine premium.

God loves covenant but hates covenant breaking: *"The men who have violated my covenant and have not fulfilled the terms of the covenant they made before me, I will treat like the calf they cut in two and then walked between its pieces"* (see Jer. 34:18).

A covenant requires sacrifice and marriage is about sacrificially laying down our personal way of life. It should reflect the oneness of the Godhead and the mystery of the trinity of God. It closely mirrors the trinity of the Godhead: the man, woman, and divinity in partnership. Entering into the marriage covenant means de-emphasizing the spirit of self-ness in reputation, interests, and opinions for the oneness of the relationship. It takes a double death to bring about a single family life. If one life holds on to its self-ness, the center may not hold.

The Married Life

The true perspective of Christian love.

Love is the crucial factor in a marriage covenant. Christian love is not blind—love that is blind is lust. Lust is an emotion that ends in a choice, while love is a decision or a choice that ends in an emotion. If a relationship starts from an emotional realm, it will lead to a choice based on emotion; therefore, the durability and strength of such a choice will depend on what feels good. It comes easily and goes quickly.

In a Christian life, choice should be first so that the emotion that develops will be based on a quality choice, a product of a valued judgment. We have been given the ability to decide to love, and this is why the Lord commands us to love one another. Emotion, on the other hand, is a feeling and cannot be commanded.

Single Christians

Single Christians planning to get married should examine each other's goals and God's calling before entering into a marriage covenant. You should pay particular attention to the weaknesses that you may have to put up with, as they may not necessarily change. Dr. Mike Murdock, senior pastor of The Wisdom Center in Texas, preaches that the person who speaks to the king in you should be your best friend. This should guide all singles looking for life partners. I have heard Pastor Jentezen Franklin, senior pastor of Free Chapel in Georgia, identify five keys to look for before marriage: spiritual compatibility, character compatibility, emotional compatibility, good communication, and mutual and physical and sexual attraction. If you cannot get these things right, maybe you should look for another!

> Lust is an emotion that ends in a choice, while love is a decision (a choice) that ends in an emotion.

Warning Signs

There are various signs of impending spiritual compromises and sexual sins that single Christians should watch out for, including:

1. Uncontrolled lustfulness, which can degenerate and become overwhelming.

    In the course of time, Amnon son of David fell in love with Tamar, the beautiful sister of Absalom son of David. Amnon became so obsessed with his sister Tamar that he made himself ill. She was a virgin, and it seemed impossible for him to do anything to her (2 Samuel 13:1-2).

2. Influence of shrewd friends, these are usually non-Christian acquaintances.

    Now Amnon had an adviser named Jonadab son of Shimeah, David's brother. Jonadab was a very shrewd man. He asked Amnon, "Why do you, the king's son, look so haggard morning after morning? Won't you tell me?" Amnon said to him, "I'm in love with Tamar, my brother Absalom's sister." "Go to bed and pretend to be ill," Jonadab said. "When your father comes to see you, say to him, 'I would like my sister Tamar to come and give me something to eat. Let her prepare the food in my sight so I may watch her and then eat it from in her hand'" (2 Samuel 13:3-5).

3. Conditions that may lead to compromise.

    *Then she took the pan and served him the bread, but he refused to eat. "**Send everyone out of here**," Amnon said. So everyone left him. Then Amnon said to Tamar, "**Bring the food here into my bedroom so I may eat from your hand**." And Tamar took the bread she had prepared and brought it to her brother Amnon in his bedroom. But when she took it to him to eat, he grabbed her and said, "Come to bed with me, my sister"* (2 Samuel 13:9-11).

4. Dealing with a sexually aroused person.

    Do not negotiate with a sexually aroused person, it is often futile. You may need to leave the place as fast as you can. The hormones are in control, not the brain. For such a person, the switch-off button is almost impossible to find. After the hormones wear out, reality sets in;

No, my brother!" she said to him. "Don't force me! Such a thing should not be done in Israel! Don't do this wicked thing. What about me? Where could I get rid of my disgrace? And what about you? You would be like one of the wicked fools in Israel. Please speak to the king; he will not keep me from being married to you." But he refused to listen to her, and since he was stronger than she, he raped her. Then Amnon hated her with intense hatred. In fact, he hated her more than he had loved her. Amnon said to her, "Get up and get out!" "No!" she said to him. "Sending me away would be a greater wrong than what you have already done to me." But he refused to listen to her. He called his personal servant and said, "Get this woman out of my sight and bolt the door after her." So his servant put her out and bolted the door after her. She was wearing an ornate robe, for this was the kind of garment the virgin daughters of the king wore. Tamar put ashes on her head and tore the ornate robe she was wearing. She put her hands on her head and went away, weeping aloud as she went (2 Samuel 13:12-19).

Married to the wrong person? Not necessarily so.

Many married people today believe they are married to the wrong person. There are no wrong persons. There are only some partners who require a lot more adjustment to reach oneness; unfortunately for some, it may take close to a lifetime. However, nothing happens by chance. Sometimes God may choose to confront us with the very thing we are trying to run from by using the person we cannot run from to shape our character.

> Sometimes God may choose to confront us with the very thing we are trying to run from by using the person we cannot run from to shape our character.

Remember, all the days of our lives were recorded in His book before anyone came to being. It is also true that our times are in His hands. Jeremiah 18:1-4 illustrates God's marvelous second chance, His circumstantial will, and how He molds us even after we have blown it with the second chance, *"shaping it as seemed best to Him."* His best is more than enough.

Partners together in receiving God's blessing.

There is hidden gold in every marriage, which is custommade. It is the responsibility of the man and woman to dig hard in order to find the winning combination that is needed to access this hidden treasure. Remember that you and your wife are partners in receiving God's blessing (see 1 Pet. 3:7).

Partners should walk beside each other and be friends through thick and thin. When the going gets tough, remind each other of what God has promised both of you. Do not be afraid to acknowledge limitation, for you cannot determine the areas of strength without first accepting the areas of weakness. It is the realization that all flesh will fail that makes each of us lean on God and find in Him what we could not find in anyone else.

Preparation for Married Life

No amount of preparation can be adequate for what you really find when you get into the realities of a marriage covenant. Both parties are ill prepared and it's usually the man who is least prepared! The only education that men will usually receive with interest and hidden enthusiasm is the area of sex education. Most men can, therefore, come into marriage sexually minded but, important as this is, it is the least thing of all that keeps a marriage strong and holy. When the excitement wears out, the reality settles in.

> "I hate divorce," says God.

> *"I hate divorce," says the Lord God of Israel,*
> *"and I hate a man's covering himself with vio-*
> *lence as well as with his garment," says the Lord*
> *Almighty. So guard yourself in your spirit, and*
> *do not break faith* (Malachi 2:16).

This is God's immutable stand on this subject. It is unquestionable and absolute, although I am aware that many have to grapple with the inevitability of this bitter issue. However, as much as it depends on you, hang on to the precepts of God. Like David said, *"I was young and now I am old, yet I have never seen the righteous forsaken or their children begging bread"* (Ps. 37:25).

It is God's requirement for us to work it out, no matter what. Sometimes this may not seem fair, but the emblem of the cross is the unfairness of humanity and the grace of divinity. Bad things happen to good people, and good things happen to bad people; but there is a God who looks over the affairs of all. If divorce happens, despite doing all you know to do, then know that this is not the end of life. God will make a way where there seems to be no way.

Adjusting to Your Partner's Personality Traits

I've noticed that the period it takes to adjust to a partner in marriage may vary greatly, and this depends on the personality types of those in the marriage. Simply put, a spouse is likely to be one of the following personality types: a friend, a mother or father, a daughter or son, or very rarely, an equal combination of any two types. No one type is better than the other. However, some personality types are more readily adjustable than others. It is crucially important that you discover the personality traits of your spouse; otherwise, you will forever be expecting the impossible.

1. *The friend type* – Great in courtship, operates on equality basis, handles joint ventures very well. Submission is often a big problem; the marriage relationship tends to be like a boat with two captains if care is not taken.

2. *The mother or father type* – Very caring, gets everything planned ahead of time. However, the partner often feels overwhelmed with too much attention and looks for the slightest opportunity to escape. It is not uncommon for this personality type to try to influence high-level professional decisions of the partner, even when he or she is a layperson in the area.

3. *The daughter or son type* – Very caring and trusting. Prefers to wait for the partner's view or decision even when they are better placed to do it. Sometimes this personality is submissive to a fault.

Submission needs to be coupled with useful contributions in the management of family issues.

On the whole, the essence is to try not to change your partner but to instead learn to enjoy and accept those things that cannot change.

DESTINY DELIBERATIONS

1. "When two people are married, they bring memories of their experiences into the marriage, which shape the way in which they understand the world, their partner, and the marriage."

   Question: How have your spouse's "memories" affected your marriage?

   _____

   _____

   Question: How have your "memories" affected your marriage?

   _____

   _____

2. "We have been given the ability to decide to love, and this is why the Lord commands us to love one another."

   Question: Is it harder to "decide to love" some people more than others?

   _____

   _____

   Question: Why is that?

   _____

   _____

3. "A spouse is likely to be one of the following personality types: a friend, a mother or father, a daughter or son, or very rarely, an equal combination of any two types."

   Question: What personality type are you? Your spouse?

   _____

   _____

Chapter 10

Responsibilities and Needs in Marriage

THIS chapter looks at the responsibilities and needs within a marriage, and specifically discusses the individual aspects of the husband and wife's roles.

The Responsibilities of Man

Paul has described in Ephesians 5:23-33 (NKJV) what some of men's responsibilities are:

Ephesians 5:23: *"For the husband is the head of the wife, as also Christ is head of the church."* The head coordinates the functions of the body and a man's ability to serve is the basis of this headship as referred to by Paul. However, the authority with which the husband is the head of the home is dependent on his ability to serve. He is accountable for the things that happen in the home, although the woman actually runs the house; therefore, he leads by example only. He should be dependable and committed to the success of the marriage. Practically, these roles are negotiated according to a husband or wife's abilities.

Ephesians 5:23b: *"And He is the Savior of the body."* Jesus Christ saved us from sins, from the dangers of this world and from the flames of eternal condemnation. The husband should empower the wife to break free from any form of oppression, both in and out of the marriage. The husband should be a source of encouragement, help, and motivation.

Ephesians 5:24: *"Therefore, just as the church is subject to Christ, so let the wives be to their own husbands in everything."* Most husbands would like their wives to be submissive to them just as the Church is to Jesus. However, the submission of wives does not imply any inferiority or lack of value, and this type of submission is not demanded. It can only be willingly given and it applies to what is fitting and proper. Christ is patient toward the Church; Christ keeps His promises; Christ is faithful and His strength is made manifest in the weaknesses of the Church. Every husband should strive to attain these standards in relation to his wife. We are commanded in Colossians 3:12 to *"...clothe yourselves with compassion, kindness, humility, gentleness and patience.*" Always. The submission of a wife will be a by-product of these virtues in the husband.

Ephesians 5:25: "*Husbands, love your wives just as Christ also loved the church and gave Himself for her.*" It's obvious that all married men have wives, but only those who love their wives qualify as husbands. Proverbs 30:21-23 says, "*Under three things the earth trembles…an unloved woman who is married.*" Therefore, a husband must not only love the wife; he must love her just as Christ loved the Church, so much so that He gave His life for her. This type of love calls for self-sacrifice:

> *Love is patient, love is kind. It does not envy, it does not boast, it is not proud. It is not rude, it is not self-seeking, it is not easily angered, it keeps no record of wrongs. Love does not delight in evil but rejoices with the truth* (1 Corinthians 13:4-6).

This is an important challenge for husbands. His love must be utterly selfless and sacrificial, devoid of bitterness, resentment, or anger.

Ephesians 5:26: "*That he might sanctify and cleanse her with the washing of water by the word.*" To sanctify means to make clean—it is not how quarrelsome or nagging your wife is but how you have succeeded in enabling her to change these and other premarital problems. To sanctify also means to set apart. Your wife should have a special place in your heart and be set apart and protected from the pressures of the world.

Ephesians 5:27: *"That he might present her to Himself a glorious church, not having spots or wrinkle or any such thing, but that she should be holy and without blemish."*

Without blemish means radiant, perfect, pure, and without blame. This is a follow-up to verse 26; the husband should enhance the potential for the wife to become presentable, regardless of what she was before they were married.

Ephesians 5:29a: *"For no one ever yet hated his own flesh, but nourishes it and cherishes it, just as the Lord does the church."* To hate your wife is to hate your own body, mind, emotion, and will. Think about this. The husband should be a source of nourishment physically and emotionally, and by so doing he will earn his wife's respect.

Ephesians 5:29b: *"Cherishes it."* This means to hold in high esteem. To cherish a wife is to make her feel important and appreciated. This feeling removes insecurity. It could be said that most women resort to nagging and jealousy as an expression of insecurity. Insecurity can lead to an inferiority complex and this leads to bitterness, anger, and depression. An insecure wife fights everything around her husband.

Here are two more important Bible verses on this issue of men and their responsibilities as husbands:

> *Husbands, in the same way be considerate as*
> *you live with your wives, and treat them with*
> *respect as the weaker partner and as heirs with*
> *you of the gracious gift of life, so that nothing*
> *will hinder your prayers* (1 Peter 3:7).

Honor your wife as co-heir to the grace of life. To be considerate means to establish good communication with your wife, as communication is the basis of understanding. The Bible calls Christian men to be students of the knowledge of the wife. If you want her to be a lady, treat her as a lady.

> *If anyone does not provide for his relatives,*
> *and especially for his immediate family, he has*
> *denied the faith and is worse than an unbeliever*
> (1 Timothy 5:8).

A man should provide for his household. This may also include encouraging the wife to provide, if she is good at doing so. If the wife is a better provider for the family, then she needs the continual encouragement and blessing of her husband. Some men may be prone to insecurity in these kinds of circumstances, and the way it is handled usually reflects the spiritual maturity of the couple.

The **Needs** of a Wife

The majority of men have no idea what the basic needs of a wife are, so here are a few pointers:

- A woman needs a man after God's heart. She needs to know and respect her husband as a man of God, as this will bring security to her spirit. It is reassuring for a wife to know that her husband hears the voice of God on a regular basis, and this can feel even better if he shares it with her.

- A wife needs intimacy and to be able to share the secrets of her husband. This often revolves around communication skills. Men are not always open to successful communication, particularly with their wives.

- Men often love to talk about high-flown subjects that have no direct bearing with their immediate environment, whereas women like to talk about the details of the immediate family. It can also be said that a man's desire is to undress his wife physically and a woman's desire is to undress her man emotionally. Women also grieve softly and heal slowly, but men grieve hard and heal fast; and men usually prefer to deal with facts and figures while women deal with feelings.

- A wife needs consistent affection: women appreciate being touched and cared for without having sexual advances made at them. A wife wants to know that she is important to her husband, but many husbands may assume and take this for granted.

- A wife needs a husband who will encourage her to find her rightful place in the Body of Christ.

- A wife needs a husband who will boost her self-esteem with encouragement and praises.

The Responsibilities of a Woman

The only person who was created as a woman was Eve: *"This is now bone of my bones and flesh of my flesh; she shall be called 'woman,' for she was taken out of man"* (Gen. 2:23). All other women were born female. Jesus said, *"Haven't you read… that at the beginning the Creator 'made them male and female'"* (Matt. 19:4). The truth is that womanhood is attained.

Let's look at Genesis 2:18:

"It is not good for a man to be alone." This does not necessarily connote loneliness (though there may be a bit of that), but is says that a man who is alone is not fully developed. Character can only be developed during the process of interaction

with other people. A woman, therefore, brings the fullness of a man to completion.

"I will make a helper [helpmate]…" God created the woman to help, protect, aid, and nurture the man to fullness.

"…suitable for him." A woman is anointed to be the specific helpmate that a husband requires. This does not depend on intelligence or physical strength but on divine ordination.

Let us now look at Proverbs 31:10-31 (NKJV) for further responsibilities of a woman in marriage:

Proverbs 31:10: *"Who can find a virtuous woman? For her worth is far above rubies."* She is a rare treasure. She is virtuous, a woman of power and strength of character. She is invaluable and worth far more than rubies.

Proverbs 31:11a: *"The heart of her husband safely trusts her."* He trusts in her fidelity to his interests and that she will never betray his counsels or have any interest separate from that of his family.

Proverbs 31:12: *"She does him good and not evil all the days of her life."* She is good to him always, in sickness, in health, in adversity, and in old age.

Proverbs 31:13a: *"She seeks wool and flax."* She is industrious.

Proverbs 31:14: *"She is like the merchant ships, she brings her food from afar."* She goes out of her way to prepare good things for her husband.

Proverbs 31:15: *"She also rises while it is yet night, and provides food for her household, and a portion for her maidservants."* She is disciplined and diligent in every household duty, economic and yet liberal, faithful, and loving as a wife and as a mother, with the fear of God in her heart.

Proverbs 31:16a: *"She considers a field and buys it."* She is prudent and provides for the growing needs of the family.

Proverbs 31:17a: *"She girds herself with strength."* She is hard working.

Proverbs 31:20a: *"She extends her hand to the poor."* She gives to the poor and needy.

Proverbs 31:23a: *"Her husband is known in the gates."* Her husband is renowned because her diligence and amiability at home enable him to attend to his public functions.

Proverbs 31:2a5: *"Strength* [of mind] *and honor are her clothing."* She is strong and noble in character.

Proverbs 31:26a: *"She opens her mouth with wisdom."* She is wise and kind. She is not talkative, but thoughtful and sensible in her words instead.

Proverbs 31:27: *"She watches over the ways of her household, and does not eat the bread of idleness."* She is not lazy.

Proverbs 31:28: *"Her children rise up and call her blessed; her husband also, and he praises her."* The children are brought up in the ways of the Lord and they, and her husband, praise her.

Here are additional responsibilities of a wife:

- She is to intercede for her family in prayers. She makes herself available to become the closest friend and the confidant of her husband. *"The wise woman builds her house, but with her own hands the foolish one tear hers down"* (Prov. 14:1). She creates a joyful atmosphere in her household; it is usually the woman who dictates the atmosphere in a home.

- *"Better to live on a corner of the roof than share a house with a quarrelsome wife"* (Prov. 21:9; 25:24). Men respond to spoken words; therefore, a woman who has got too much to say will drive her husband to the rooftop. Even though he may physically sleep in the marriage bed, his heart could be on the roof or somewhere else.

- *"Your desire will be for your husband, and he will rule over you"* (Gen. 3:16b). This is an obligation to the home. It should be the joy of a woman's responsibility to her husband:

  Your beauty should not come from outward adornment, such as braided hair and the wearing of gold jewelry and fine clothes. Instead, it should be that of your inner self, the unfading beauty of a gentle and quiet spirit, which is of great worth in God's sight. For this is the way the holy woman of the past who put their hope in God used to make herself beautiful. They were submissive to their husbands, like Sarah, who obeyed Abraham and called him her master. You are her daughters if you do what is right and do not give way to fear (1 Peter 3:3-6).

The Needs of a Husband

- A man needs a wife who is just as zealous about God as he is.

- A husband needs respect from his wife. If a man does not get respect from his wife, it drains him and dampens his desire to prove his manliness. A wife should esteem her husband, otherwise she becomes a hindrance to the expression of his manliness. This can happen in the following ways:

1. Using exciting words to describe other people that she has never used when speaking about her husband. It is devaluating and disrespectful.

2. By resisting his decisions and emphasizing her point by bringing up his wrong decisions in the past.

3. By resisting his spirit through the spirit of rebellion. Negative vibrations can be sent out in quiet and very subtle ways.

4. By resisting his physical affection or advances. Resisting his sexual advances crushes a man's spirit.

   • A man needs a wife who will be loyal to him through thick and thin, particularly at his worst moments. Encouragement from his wife can easily change a man.

   • A man needs a wife who listens and pays attention to him.

   • A husband needs a wife who appreciates and shows gratitude for what he has done, as well as what he has refused to be involved in; those things which may be a common problem among other men.

   • A husband needs a wife who is devoted to him.

DESTINY DELIBERATIONS

1. "A husband's love must be utterly selfless and sacrificial, devoid of bitterness, resentment, or anger."

   Question: If you are a husband, how hard is this statement to live?

   _____

   _____

   Question: Is it even possible?

   _____

   _____

2. "Men often love to talk about high-flown subjects that have no direct bearing with their immediate environment, whereas women like to talk about the details of the immediate family."

   Question: Is this a true statement regarding your personal experience?

   _____

   _____

3. "A wife should esteem her husband; otherwise, she becomes a hindrance to the expression of his manliness."

   Question: If you are a wife, have you witnessed this negative consequence in your marital relationship?

   _____

   _____

Chapter 11

Fundamentals for a
Successful Marriage

THIS chapter is devoted solely to providing you specifics about how to have a successful and enjoyable marriage. I have included a husband and wife checklist, problem areas to be mindful of, wise key points, the importance of communication, and specific steps to take to resolve conflict.

First, the checklist and scorecard:

	Husband	Wife	Scale (0 min to +5 max)
Principle need	To be respected, especially in public	To be cherished	_____
Principle command	Love your wife	Submit to your husband	_____
Principle strength	Crowned with anointing to head the family	Humility for victory	_____
			Scale (-5 max to 0 min)
	_____	_____	
Cardinal disobedience	Not to love the wife	Not to submit	_____
Main weakness	Pride— usually the result of hidden fear	Over-reaction	_____
Common temptations	Anger and lust	Fear and insecurity	_____
Total score	_____	_____	_____

(A) Self-check: *On a scale of 0 to 5 for virtues and -5 to 0 for vices, score yourself and see the author's interpretation of the score at the end of this chapter.*

There are many problem areas in marriage that you should be aware of and address as soon as possible. Here are some of the common ones:

- Lack of communication _____
- Lack of intimacy _____
- Failure to bear with one another _____
- The pressures of the needs of a growing family _____
- Financial pressure _____
- Lack of tolerance _____
- Abuse: physical, mental or sexual _____
- Insult: unkind words that shake confidence _____
- Neglect: to ignore _____
- Guilt: by-product of experience _____
- Failing to translate your differences into strengths _____

(B) Self-check: *On a scale 'yes' (+1) if the problem area exists; and 'no' (0) if the problem does not exist, score yourself and check the author's interpretation at the end of this chapter.*

Key Points

The following should be seriously considered. They are key points to being wise in your marriage, which will lead to a loving and devoted-to-each-other relationship:

1. Touch each other as often as possible. _____

2. Spend time together. _____

3. Encourage each other with kind words. _____

4. Love and accept yourselves without conditions. A happy couple does not believe that they have to perform to be accepted. _____

5. Commit to each other. _____

6. Take care of your financial future together; money creates the most common stress in marriage. _____

7. Engage or entertain yourselves with lively humor; the joy of the Lord is your strength. _____

8. Make your spouse the top of your priorities. _____

9. Make efforts to please each other. _____

10. Pray together; if you pray together, you stick together. _____

11. Be tolerant of your partner's weaknesses and do not expect an overnight change. _____

12. Forgiving each other: Forgiveness is an act of grace and not a reward for good behavior. _____

13. Trusting each other: Trust is a process not an event; therefore it takes time to build. Make yourself trustworthy regardless. _____

14. Avoid the spirit of control by manipulation or intimidation; this is the spirit of witchcraft. _____

15. Do not use children to provoke your partner. _____

16. Do not dwell on the weaknesses of your partner, or you will soon be infected with the same spirit: *"as a man thinks in own heart, so he is."* _____

17. Avoid trying to change your partner into a person of your lust. _____

18. Be mindful of your pronouncements: some truths are bitter, but good timing may help. _____

19. Harbor no evil thoughts against your partner. Such imaginations are spiritual knives in the hands of the devil. _____

20. Keep a "golden silence"; a tongue that is bridled must be accompanied by a mind that is controlled. Your thoughts have to align with your confession, otherwise your house is divided against itself. A silence that is not golden is dangerous because outwardly everything appears nice and smooth,

but beneath the surface is a mind of turmoil, aggravation, and a flaming inferno, a built-up pressure that is itching to explode. A passion that is not expressed leads to perversion and destruction. If you cannot control your mind, then speak out, confront the situation, and get help. Silence is golden if the mind is controlled and the tongue is bridled. _____

(C) Self-Check: *On a scale of 'yes' (1) if the key point is happening and 'no' (0) if you are working on it or struggling with it, score yourself and check the author's interpretation at the end of the chapter.*

Communication and Resolving Marital Conflicts

Communication

Where there is union, there is always some form of communication. However, this can be either effective or ineffective. A lack of effective communication does not just mean an absence of talking; it means not talking about anything of importance. This can lead to misunderstanding and a feeling of being neglected, being ignored, and the loss of self-esteem.

The habit of listening needs to be cultivated. Most people need someone who will listen to them, not just someone who will talk to them. You need someone with whom you feel safe enough to share your heart. Listening gives your partner a sense of dignity and value, so don't just listen with "ears" as some people pretend to do, but stop what you are doing, ask appropriate questions, and give encouraging signals.

Resolving Conflicts in Marriage

Conflicts happen in a marriage. The wisdom is in knowing how to deal with them when they occur. You should learn to resolve the conflict between yourselves, and you should always start with doing what you can to help resolve the issue, such as self-adjustment, increasing your level of tolerance, forgiveness where necessary and, of course, looking up to Jesus. Often, other people find it easier to adjust when you have taken the first step in making the adjustment.

> Christian marriage is not the absence of conflict but the understanding of it.

God's basis for fellowship is to come together and reason. Christian marriage is not the absence of conflict but the understanding of it. If conflict is not resolved, you become resentful and bitter, and this bitterness defiles the marriage.

Determine not to be hurtful, but develop mutual respect and try to keep to this, no matter what. Do not be eager to attack your partner with harsh words and never, ever get aggressive or physical. If something has already been dealt with, do not drag it up in order to make a point; stick to the issue at hand. Try also to learn how to lose an argument, because it is very frustrating to live with a partner who is (or thinks he or she is) always right. Remember, the aim is to get closer and not just to win an argument.

Steps to resolve conflict:

- Seek the counsel of God. _____
- Identify the problem. _____
- Find the root source of the problem. _____
- Put a high premium on what you can do on your part. _____
- Evaluate the situation in a considerate manner. _____
- Find mutually acceptable terms. _____
- Negotiate around these terms and come to a workable agreement. _____

(D) Self-check: *On a scale of 'yes' (1) if the step occurs in your conflict resolution and 'no' (0) if it does not, score yourself and see the author's interpretation at the end of this chapter.*

Unfortunately, these days there are just as many divorces among believers as nonbelievers. As children of God, we have a special privilege of honoring our heavenly Father through our marriages. The following chapters discuss the roles of Christian men and women and how critical they are to success in every aspect of life.

DESTINY DELIBERATIONS

1. How many "problem areas" did you identify from the list that are evident in your marriage?

   _____

   _____

2. How many "key points" are you going to instill into your daily relationship with your spouse?

   _____

   _____

3. "Remember, the aim is to get closer and not just to win an argument."

    Question: Do you lose sight of this truth when you are in a heated discussion with your spouse?

    _____

    _____

    Question: What can you do to keep the goal of closeness in sight instead?

    _____

    _____

(A) 0 to 1= average score, need to improve; 2 = good; 3 = very good and 4-5 = probably need to be honest with yourself

_____

_____

(B) Less than 3 = doing fairly well; 3 to 5 needs to work on the relationship and greater than 5 = moving into danger zone

_____

_____

(C) Less than 10 = needs to improve on the relationship; 10 = fair; 10 to 15 = doing well and 20 = sincerity is probably an issue

_____

_____

(D) Greater than 2 = success will eventually come and 2 or less than 2 = danger zone

Chapter 12

The Attributes of a Christian Man

From the Cradle to a Man of God

M ANHOOD is attained through the varying degrees of success in the challenges of life. A man is not what he does, but what he stands for, and this choice of becoming a man is open to every male.

Jesus epitomizes all that it takes to be a man. In Him we see courage, righteousness, firmness, and compassion. He wept when it was unavoidable, He was bold enough to lay down His life for our sins, He rebuked the "teachers of law" for hypocrisy, and He single-handedly drove out the traders from the house of God. Yet, He was also merciful enough to ask forgiveness for those who crucified Him.

Jonathan was the eldest and favorite son of King Saul. He was a courageous, capable, and manly warrior. He deserved being described as *"swifter than the eagles"* and *"stronger than lions"* (see 2 Sam. 1:23), and he was skilled as an archer (see 1 Sam. 20:20). He was especially endeared to Saul, but this did not overshadow Jonathan's zeal for God.

Jonathan is noted mainly for his unselfish friendship and support for David as God's King designated and fought to his death, dying on the same day as his father and two of his brothers. However, Jonathan died in the wrong house and, for all his good qualities and achievements, he died in the house that the spirit of God had left.

> Jesus epitomizes all that it takes to be a man.

Men should stand up for their convictions. You should not, out of respect for anybody, be where God has left. Do not die in an in-between situation like Jonathan did. Stand firm for your convictions.

David is another example of the true man, *"I have found David the son of Jesse, a man after Mine own heart, who will do all My will"* (Acts 13:22 NKJV). This shepherd, musician, poet, soldier, statesman, prophet, and king stands out with great prominence. He was a fierce fighter on the battlefield and showed endurance under hardship; he was a leader and commander, strong and unwavering in courage, yet humble enough to acknowledge his mistakes, repenting for his adulterous affair with Bathsheba. He was also capable of tender compassion and mercy, a lover of truth and righteousness and, above all, he had implicit trust and confidence in God.

The Male Child

Samuel was one of those who committed to the service of God at a tender age. He was taken to the tabernacle of Shiloh upon being weaned at the age of three years as a Nazarene, and he was left there under the guidance of the high priest, Eli. As the Bible records, he "ministered to God" as a boy, and as he grew into manhood he "continued to grow in stature and in favor with the Lord and with men" (1 Sam. 2:26).

Josiah was eight years old when he became king (see 2 Kings 22:1). He reigned for thirty-one years in Jerusalem, and he did what was right in the sight of the Lord, walking in all the ways of his father, David. Josiah did not turn aside to the right hand or to the left. Josiah ruled Judah after the notorious regime of Manassah.

> Stand firm for your convictions.

At the age of twelve years, Jesus asked His parents, "Did you not know that I must be about my father's business?" (Luke 2:49 NKJV).

For the male child, the following are worthy of note:

> *Children, obey your parents in the Lord, for this is right. Honor your father and mother which is the first commandment with a promise that it may go well with you and that you may enjoy long life on the earth* (Ephesians 6:1-3).

> *Do not rebuke an older man harshly, but exhort him as if he were your father* (1 Timothy 5:1a).

> *Don't let anyone look down on you because you are young, but set an example for the believers in speech, in life, in love, in faith and in purity* (1 Timothy 4:12).

> *But the Lord said to me, "Do not say, 'I am only a child.' You must go to everyone I send you to and say whatever I command you"* (Jeremiah 1:7).

If the Lord sends you, He will give you the wisdom to carry His purpose out, irrespective of your age:

> *Flee the evil desires of youth, and pursue right-eousness, faith, love and peace, along with those*

who call on the Lord out of a pure heart. And the Lord's servant must not quarrel; instead, he must be kind to everyone, able to teach, not resentful (2 Timothy 2:22,24).

Transiting to Manhood

The Bible says that the sons of Issachar were men who had an understanding of the times; they knew what Israel ought to do and all their brethren were at their command (see 1 Chron. 12:32). Like these sons of Issachar, you need to understand the timing and season of the Spirit of God, then you will know when to assume the responsibilities of manhood and know when you are called to leadership.

It was at such transitory phase that David said to Solomon, *"I am about to go the way of all the earth,"* he said. ***"So be strong, show yourself a man, and observe what the Lord your God requires:*** *Walk in His ways, and keep His decrees and commands, His laws and requirements, as written in the Law of Moses, so that you may prosper in all you do and wherever you go"* (1 Kings 2:2-3).

In a similar circumstance, the Lord said to Joshua, *"Moses my servant is dead. Now then, you and all these people, get ready to cross the Jordan River into the land I am about to give them. Be strong and very courageous…"* (Joshua 1:2,7).

These two examples illustrate the call into manhood, showing its characteristics of timing and responsibilities.

Christians in Partnership

Man's pursuits on earth are done in association, partnership, or collaboration with other people. In any such associations, *"Each one* [participant] *should use whatever gift he has received to serve others, faithfully administering God's grace in its various forms"* (1 Peter 4:10).

There are various forms of partnership, but they all fall into one of two groups—evil or good. Evil partnerships lead to destruction, but the good ones lead to fruition. However, any partnership that is not based on Jesus Christ will not stand the test of time. For the Bible says that unless the Lord builds a house, the laborers labor in vain (see Ps. 127:1).

In Ecclesiastes 4:9, it says that *"two are better than one,"* and a cord of three strands cannot be easily broken. The third strand in a godly partnership is Jesus, the rock of ages. Alliances can be formed in various ways through marriage, in war, in business, and in Christian fellowship.

- Alliance for warfare.

Now Jehoshaphat had great wealth and honor, and he allied himself with Ahab by marriage. Some years later he went down to visit Ahab in Samaria. …Ahab king of Israel asked Jehoshaphat king of Judah, "Will you go with me against Ramoth Gilead?" Jehoshaphat replied, "I am as you are, and my people as your people; we will join you in the war" (2 Chronicles 18:1-4).

However, King Ahab was evil, and so God rebuked Jehoshaphat saying, *"Should you help the wicked and love those who hate the Lord?"* (2 Chron. 19:2). This partnership was evil because it was not based on God. It led to the death of King Ahab, but Jehoshaphat was spared after being admonished.

• Alliance for trade.

Later, Jehoshaphat king of Judah made an alliance with Ahaziah, king of Israel, who was guilty of wickedness. He agreed with him to construct a fleet of trading ships (2 Chronicles 20:35-36a).

Ahaziah was an evil king and this was an evil and ill-fated partnership. Because of this, God prophesied against Jehoshaphat saying, *"Because you have made an alliance with Ahaziah, the Lord will destroy what you have made." The ships were wrecked and were not able to set sail to trade"* (2 Chron.

20:37). The Bible says in First Corinthians 15:33, *"Do not be misled: Bad company corrupts good character."*

The Man as a Father

This is a topic that is assuming greater and greater significance in our generation as more and more men are growing up without fathers in their homes. As a result, they are denied the privilege of a role model. The truth is that God knows everything and He is able to teach and train men to be godly fathers. His grace is sufficient for all situations.

The Bible says:

> *Fathers, do not exasperate your children; instead, bring them up in the training and instruction of the Lord* (Ephesians 6:4).

> *Train a child in the way he should go, and when he is old he will not turn from it* (Proverbs 22:6).

The Christian in the Workplace

The Bible has a lot to say about Christians and the workplace. There are basic principles that will make you successful and respected if you take seriously what the Bible says.

If a man will not work, he shall not eat (2 Thessalonians 3:10).

Serve wholeheartedly, as if you were serving the Lord, not men, because you know that the Lord will reward everyone for whatever good he does... (Ephesians 6:7-8).

Do your best to present yourself to God as one approved, a workman who does not need to be ashamed... (2 Timothy 2:15).

And masters, treat your slaves in the same way. Do not threaten them, since you know that He who is both their Master and yours is in heaven, and there is no favoritism with Him (Ephesians 6:9).

Everyone must submit himself to governing authorities, for there is no authority except that which God has established. The authorities that exist have been established by God. Consequently, he who rebels against the authority is rebelling against what God has instituted... (Romans 13:1-2).

The Christian in Church

The wisdom in the Bible also includes a Christian man's behavior as a member of the Body of Christ:

> *Do not let this Book of the Law depart from your mouth; mediate on it day and night, so that you may be careful to do everything written in it. Then you will be prosperous and successful* (Joshua 1:8).

> *If you have any encouragement from being united with Christ, if any comfort from His love, if any fellowship with the Spirit, if any tenderness and compassion, then make my joy complete by being like-minded, having the same love, being one in spirit and purpose. Do nothing out of selfish ambition or vain conceit, but in humility consider others better than yourselves. Each of you should look not only to your own interests, but also to the interests of others* (Philippians 2:1-4).

Keep on loving each other as brothers [in fellowship] (Hebrews 13:1).

Speak to one another with psalms, hymns and spiritual songs. Sing and make music in your heart to the Lord, always giving thanks to God the Father for everything, in the name of our Lord Jesus Christ. Submit to one another out of reverence for Christ (Ephesians 5:19-21).

Therefore, as God's chosen people, holy and dearly loved, clothe yourselves with compassion, kindness, humility, gentleness and patience. Bear with each other and forgive whatever grievances you may have against one another. Forgive as the Lord forgave you. And over all these virtues put on love, which binds them all together in perfect unity (Colossians 3:12-14).

As Overseer or Church Leader

Church leaders and overseers have particular responsibilities. Take advice from the ultimate Overseer:

If anyone sets his heart on being an overseer, he desires a noble task. Now the overseer must be above reproach, the husband of but one wife, temperate, self-controlled, respectable, hospitable, able to teach, not given to drunkenness, not violent but gentle, not quarrelsome, not a lover of money (1 Timothy 3:2-3).

Be shepherds of God's flock that is under your care, serving as overseers—not because you must, but because you are willing, as God wants you to be; not greedy for money, but eager to serve; not lording it over those entrusted to you, but being examples to the flock (1 Peter 5:2-3).

But you, man of God, flee from all this [love of money]*, and pursue righteousness, godliness, faith, love, endurance and gentleness. Fight the good fight of the faith* (1 Timothy 6:11-12).

All Scripture is God-breathed and is useful for teaching, rebuking, correcting and training in righteousness, so that the man of God may be thoroughly equipped for every good work (2 Timothy 3:16-17).

The Mighty Men of David

The Bible says that the army of David was like the army of the Lord:

> *All those who were in distress or in debt or discontented gathered around him, and he became their leader. About four hundred men were with him* (1 Samuel 22:2).

> *And David became more and more powerful, because the Lord Almighty was with him* (1 Chronicles 11:9).

> *They helped David against raiding bands, for all of them were brave warriors, and they were commanders in his army* (1 Chronicles 12:21).

> *All these men of war, who could keep ranks, came to Hebron with a loyal heart, to make David king over all Israel; and all the rest of*

Israel were of one mind to make David king (1 Chronicles 12:38 NKJV).

Lessons from David's army:

1. Anointed leadership draws followers.
2. They were men driven by the ills of their society.
3. They were motivated and committed to the future.
4. They had a common goal to make David king over all of Israel.
5. They found fellowship under the leadership of David.
6. They came with perfect and sincere hearts.
7. They had brotherly love.
8. They were united in spirit and in purpose.
9. They experienced promotion and became commanders themselves.
10. Other men were added to them.

These attributes of Christian men are ones we need to adopt into our lives immediately. God is pleased when believing men exude His attributes and rewards them with victory.

DESTINY DELIBERATIONS

1. "Jesus epitomizes all that it takes to be a man."

    Question: In addition to the characteristics listed at the beginning of the chapter about Jesus, what does He mean to you? Write what He means to you—identifying traits that are personally meaningful to you.

    _____

    _____

2. "This partnership was evil because it was not based on God."

   Question: Do you have partnerships at work, home, church, or in other activities that are not based on godly principles?

   _____

   _____

   Question: Would you have been a mighty man of David's army?

   _____

   _____

   Question: Are you now a mighty man of God's army?

   _____

   _____

Chapter 13

The Anointing of Womanhood

FROM Exodus to Revelation the role and influence of women is abundant in Scripture, from the mother of Moses, the prayer tears of Hannah, the courage of Deborah, and the personal sacrifice of Esther to the faithfulness and tenacity of Mary and Martha. In the second letter to Timothy, the apostle Paul said:

> *To Timothy, my dear son: Grace, mercy and peace from God the Father and Christ Jesus our Lord. I thank God, whom I serve, as my forefathers did, with a clear conscience, as night and day I constantly remember you in my prayers. Recalling your tears, I long to see you, so that*

> *I may be filled with joy. I have been reminded*
> *of your sincere faith, which first lived in your*
> *grandmother Lois and in your mother Eunice*
> *and, I am persuaded, now lives in you also*
> (2 Timothy 1:2-5).

Have you ever wondered why Paul did not mention the fathers in Timothy's lineage? This is because the influence of mothers in shaping the destiny of their children cannot be overemphasized. Truly the hands that rock the cradle rule the world. In modern times, from Africa to the Middle East to North America and in any place where women are relegated, the center does not hold and things fall apart. This is a timeless truth worthy of note.

Intercessors

Ensconced in the comfort of the palace of the powerful Persian empire was Esther, a woman of Jewish descent. In risking her life, she laid aside personal comfort and security to save her generation. Her courageous words are a classic statement of heroism, *"I will go the king, even though it is against the law. If I perish, I perish"* (Esther 4:16). This profile of courage closely mirrors the pattern for spiritual intercession. God is raising up an army of Esthers, an army of bridal intercessors, and these intercessors need to take their places before the coming move of apostolic restoration can be fully positioned.

Esther's petition moved the Persian king because of her place in an intimate relationship. The need for womanhood to move closer to God for unbroken communion with divinity is crucial in the days in which we live. This will fully unravel the spiritual watchfulness and discernment that is inherent in the nature of womanhood.

The prayers offered by the army of Esther will move the heart and hands of God; then we will see the soothing effects of the balm of Gilead being released across the nations like *"the leaves of the tree of life."* The Church will also rise up to take its rightful place.

At a time of great spiritual low, economic recession, and political instability in Israel, a woman, Deborah, rose to the challenge when the men were crippled with fear. She became a judge of very renowned wisdom, a poet, a prophetess, a mother, and a wife, and she led the army to victory in the battle against better-equipped oppressors. Deborah was, therefore, one of the most balanced characters—male or female—in the Bible. Any woman can stand up to be counted in her generation! I encourage you to join the bridal intercessors of the

> The prayers offered by the army of Esther will move the heart and hands of God.

new order of Esther and the warriors of the victorious army of Deborah.

The Birthing of Spiritual Pregnancies

Bringing delivery to the many spiritual pregnancies requires a *"birthing process."* Who is better placed to do this than a virtuous woman? In the physical realm, each time a woman gives birth it is vengeance on satan because childbirth is not meant to be this painful and agonizing. As recorded in Genesis:

> *The man said, "The woman you put here with me—she gave me some fruit from the tree, and I ate it." Then the Lord God said to the woman, "What is this you have done?" The woman said, "The serpent deceived me, and I ate." So the Lord God said to the serpent, "Because you have done this, cursed are you above all the livestock and all the wild animals! You will crawl on your belly and you will eat dust all the days of your life. And I will put enmity between you and the woman, and between your offspring and hers; he will crush your head, and you will strike his heel." To the*

It is time to seek the Lord.

> *woman he said, "I will greatly increase your*
> *pains in childbearing; with pain you will give*
> *birth to children..."* (Genesis 3:12-16).

This painful childbirth has become a model for birthing spiritual pregnancies.

The call to a new order of Esther challenges women to rise up for their sons, for their daughters, for their husbands, and to rise up for the land just as Deborah did in the time when judges ruled Israel. It is time to seek the Lord. No longer is it enough to paddle in the shallow waters; it is time to move to the deep—for the miraculous catch and it is time to do something new. Remember, every *"wise woman builds her house"* (Prov. 14:1). Each house that is well-built contributes to the strength of the city and the entire army of the Lord.

When the going got tough, the prophet Jeremiah knew whom to call saying, *"Consider now! Call for the wailing women to come; send for the most skillful of them. Let them come quickly and wail over us..."* (Jer. 9:17-18). Way back in time, God also conferred special discernment of womanhood when He said, *"And I will put enmity between you* [serpent] *and the woman"* (Gen. 3:15). God later said, *"The Lord will create a new thing on earth—a woman will surround* [protect] *a man"* (Jer. 31:22b). Now is the time that a woman shall *"encompass"* a man by standing strong, no matter what.

Jesus also affirmed the spiritual *"watchman"* need of the woman over her home. In Luke 15, Jesus told three parables; 1) the parable of the lost sheep, the man went out of the home to look for the lost sheep; 2) the parable of the lost son, the man rushed out of the home to meet the returning son; and 3) the parable of the lost coin, the woman rose up and swept the house clean until she found the silver coin.

> *Or suppose a woman has ten silver coins and loses one. Does she not light a lamp, sweep the house and search carefully until she finds it? And when she finds it, she calls her friends and neighbors together and says, "Rejoice with me; I have found my lost coin"* (Luke 15:8-9).

Women will continue to make positive differences in the lives of their children, families, communities, workplaces, and nations when totally focused on God's will for their lives.

DESTINY DELIBERATIONS

1. "This is because the influence of mothers in shaping the destiny of their children cannot be overemphasized."

   Question: If you are a mother, are you aware how important your role is in shaping your children's destiny?

   _____

   _____

2. "God is raising up an army of Esther's, an army of bridal intercessors."

   Question: Are you ready to sign up?

   _____

   _____

   Question: Are you ready to take your position on the front lines of prayer?

   _____

   _____

3. "Now is the time that a woman shall "encompass" a man by standing strong, no matter what."

   Question: What does this statement mean to you?

   _____

   _____

   Question: How strong are you?

   _____

   _____

Chapter 14

There Is Power in Youthfulness

Do Not Waste Your Youthfulness

THERE are two key elements in tapping into the special anointing of youthfulness:

1. The work of the Holy Spirit.
2. Understanding the strengths and limits of youthfulness.

Anointing is the power expression of the Holy Spirit. It is the enabling power, which is divinely imparted for the purpose of fulfilling a heavenly vision. God is always looking for the arm of humankind through which to express the arm of the Lord. Youths offer availability and the abundance of youthful energy, *"The glory of young men is their strength, and the splendor of old men is their gray head"* [suggesting wisdom and experience] (Prov. 20:29 NKJV).

However, the world system is also geared toward negatively exploiting this virtue. This is why the Bible says we should remember our Creator in the days of our youth. This refers to the lost zeal that may accompany diminishing physical fitness that comes with age:

> *Remember your Creator in the days of your youth, before the days of trouble come and the years approach when you will say, "I find no pleasure in them"* (Ecclesiastes 12:1).

This speaks of remembering God before the eyes and emotions start to fail:

> *Before the sun and the light and the moon and the stars grow dark, and the clouds return after the rain* (Ecclesiastes 12:2).

Anointing is the power expression of the Holy Spirit.

Remember the Lord before the mind, the hands, the legs, and the teeth become less useful:

> *When the keepers of the house tremble, and the strong men stoop, when the grinders cease*

*because they are few, and those looking through
the windows grow dim* (Ecclesiastes 12:3).

Remember the Lord before the voice and the hearing
apparatus start to fail:

*When the doors to the streets are closed and the
sound of grinding fades; when men rise up at
the sounds of birds, but all their songs grow faint*
(Ecclesiastes 12:4).

Before the hair goes gray, the appetite fails, and morbid
fear sets in:

*When men are afraid of heights of dangers in
the streets; when the almond tree* [white hair]
*blossoms, and the grasshopper drags himself
along and desire no longer stirred. Then man
goes to his eternal home and mourners go about
the streets* (Ecclesiastes 12:5).

Remember God Almighty while you live on earth:

*Remember Him—before the silver cord is sev-
ered, or the golden bowl is broken* (Ecclesiastes
12:6).

The Word of God

Only the Word of God brings light and life to how important youth are in His plan of salvation and advancing His Kingdom on earth.

> *How can a young man keep his way pure? By living according to Your word* (Psalm 119:9).

> *Your word is a lamp to my feet and a light for my path* (Psalm 119:105).

> *Flee the evil desires of youth, and pursue righteousness, faith, love and peace, along with those who call on the Lord out of a pure heart* (2 Timothy 2:22).

Satan—the Prince of this World

Satan targets youth just as he targets adult believers. But they all should be very sure that the evil one has been conquered once and for all through the blood Jesus shed on the cross. Although satan is the ruler of this world, he has no power over any believer living a righteous life.

> *Now is the time for judgment on this world; now the prince of this world will be driven out* (John 12:31).

> *We know that we are children of God, and that the whole world is under the control of the evil one* (1 John 5:19).

This is the way that satan uses the worldly system to influence people as described in First John 2:16:

> *For everything in the world—the cravings of sinful man, the lust of his eyes and the boasting of what he has and does—comes not from the Father but from the world.*

- The cravings of a sinful man (the man living solely on natural instincts and not led by the Spirit of God), are gratifications of the flesh, such as unlawful sexual desires, excessive desires for comfort, pleasures, and fine food.

- The second weapon of the enemy is lust of the eyes. This means man's greed and covetousness.

- The third weapon of satan is a subtle but very powerful one—the pride of life. Of all human shortcomings, this is the only one that arises from the position of strength. It means taking pride in one's accomplishments, seeking a good name or a high position, and putting confidence in yourself rather than in God.

However, we should be bold and confident in God:

Don't let anyone look down on you because you are young, but set an example for the believers in speech, in life, in love, in faith and in purity. Until I come, devote yourself to the public reading of Scripture, to preaching and to teaching (1 Timothy 4:12-13).

"Ah, Sovereign Lord," I said, "I do not know how to speak; I am only a child." But the Lord said to me, "Do not say, 'I am only a child.' You must go to everyone I send you to and say whatever I command you. Do not be afraid of them, for I am with you and will rescue you," declares the Lord (Jeremiah 1:6-8).

Life is a journey full of challenges and many are daunting, but inherent in every challenge is victory wrapped up in an unattractive package and hidden, waiting for those who will dig deep enough to find it. Challenges are the precursors for victories! Trials are the testing grounds for great success.

Nehemiah was once confronted with the daunting task of rebuilding the broken walls of post-exilic Jerusalem in the midst of ridicules, threats of violence, and psychological warfare from the enemies of the Jews. In the course of his challenge, he made a classic statement that stands out for all times:

> Challenges are the precursors for victories! Trials are the testing grounds for great success.

> *I am carrying on a great project and cannot go down. Why should the work stop while I leave it and go down to you?* (Nehemiah 6:3).

This statement is as relevant for us today as it was for the people in Nehemiah's days. If you are destined for the top, don't let the issues of life bring you down. Like the eagle mounts on the storm to rise to a higher level, allow your life issues be your springboards for greater heights.

Always remember, all believers receive power from the Lord when we take steps to fulfill His plan for our lives.

DESTINY DELIBERATIONS

1. "There are two key elements in tapping into the special anointing of youthfulness: The work of the Holy Spirit and understanding the strengths and limits of youthfulness."

   Question: Whether you are a young person or someone who works with a youth ministry, knowing these two key elements are important. Why and in what ways?

   _____

   _____

2. "The world system is geared toward negatively exploiting youthfulness in the ministry."

    Question: How do you, or your church, counteract this negatively and do you proactively promote availability and youthful energy to forward the Kingdom of God?

    _____

    _____

3. "Trials are the testing grounds for great success."

    Question: Of the three weapons satan uses to influence people (fleshly cravings, lust, pride), which one do you think most tempts young people?

    _____

    _____

Conclusion

YOU are destined for the top—the top of your class, your pay grade, your ministry, your family's respect—whatever top level God's will is for your life, you can achieve it!

I hope that after reading this book, you now know how to handle the issues of life that come your way—and stand in your way—so that you can keep moving toward the top. Nothing can stop you when you are living:

- By the rules of life
- By love
- In unity
- Wisely
- Righteously
- Victoriously over sin

- Spiritually
- A life of prayer

God bless you as you journey on—upward bound!

About the Author

D<small>R. J</small>OE I<small>BOJIE</small>, founder and senior pastor of The Father's House, travels nationally and internationally as a Bible and prophetic teacher. He combines a unique prophetic gifting with rare insight into the mysteries of God and the ancient biblical methods of understanding dreams and visions. His ministry has blessed thousands by bringing down-to-earth clarity to the prophetic ministry. He is a popular speaker worldwide. He and his wife, Cynthia, live in Aberdeen, Scotland.

CONTACT INFORMATION

For additional copies of this book and other products from Cross House Books, contact: sales@crosshousebooks.co.uk.

Please visit our Website for product updates and news at www.crosshousebooks.co.uk.

OTHER INQUIRIES

CROSS HOUSE BOOKS
Christian Book Publishers
245 Midstocket Road
Aberdeen, AB15 5PH, UK

info@crosshousebooks.co.uk
publisher@crosshousebooks.co.uk

"The entrance of Your Word brings light."

MINISTRY INFORMATION

Dr. Joe Ibojie is the Senior Pastor of
THE FATHER'S HOUSE

The Father's House is a family church and a vibrant community of Christians located in Aberdeen, Scotland, UK. The Father's House seeks to build a bridge of hope across generations, racial divides, and gender biases through the ministry of the Word.

You are invited to come and worship if you are in the area.

For location, please visit the church's Website:
www.the-fathers-house.org.uk

For inquiries:
info@the-fathers-house.org.uk
Call 44 1224 701343

How to Live the Supernatural Life in the Here and Now—BEST SELLER

Are you ready to stop living an ordinary life? You were meant to live a supernatural life! God intends us to experience His power every day! In *How to Live the Supernatural Life in the Here and Now* you will learn how to bring the supernatural power of God into everyday living. Finding the proper balance for your life allows you to step into the supernatural and to move in power and authority over everything around you. Dr. Joe Ibojie, an experienced pastor and prolific writer, provides practical steps and instruction that will help you to:

- Step out of the things that hold you back in life.
- Understand that all life is spiritual.
- Experience the supernatural life that God has planned for you!
- Find balance between the natural and the spiritual.
- Release God's power to change and empower your circumstances.

Are you ready to live a life of spiritual harmony? Then you are ready to learn *How to Live the Supernatural Life in the Here and Now!*

Dreams and Visions Volume 1—BEST SELLER

Dreams and Visions presents sound scriptural principles and practical instructions to help you understand dreams and visions. The book provides readers with the necessary understanding to approach dreams and visions by the Holy Spirit through biblical illustrations, understanding of the meaning of dreams and prophetic symbolism, and by exploring the art of dream interpretation according to ancient methods of the Bible.

Dreams and Visions Volume 2—NEW

God speaks to you through dreams and visions. Do you want to know the meaning of your dreams? Do you want to know what He is telling and showing you? Now you can know!

Dreams and Visions Volume 2 is packed full of exciting and Bible-guided ways to discover the meaning of your God-inspired, dreamy nighttime adventures and your wide-awake supernatural experiences!

Dr. Joe Ibojie reveals why and how God wants to communicate with you through dreams and visions. In this *second volume*, the teaching emphasizes how to gain clearer understanding of your dreams and visions in a new, in-depth, and user-friendly way.

Illustrated Bible-Based Dictionary of Dream Symbols— BEST SELLER

Illustrated Bible-Based Dictionary of Dream Symbols is much more than a book of dream symbols. This book is a treasure chest, loaded down with revelation and the hidden mysteries of God that have been waiting since before the foundation of the earth to be uncovered. Whether you use this book to assist in interpreting your dreams or as an additional resource for your study of the Word of God, you will find it a welcome companion.

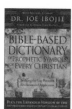

EXPANDED AND ENRICHED WITH EXCITING NEW CONTENT

Bible-Based Dictionary of Prophetic Symbols for Every Christian—NEW

The most comprehensive, illustrated Bible-based dictionary of prophetic and dream symbols ever compiled is contained in this one authoritative book!

The Bible-Based Dictionary of Prophetic Symbols for Every Christian is a masterpiece that intelligently and understandably bridges the gap between prophetic revelation and application—PLUS it includes the expanded version of the best selling *Illustrated Bible-Based Dictionary of Dream Symbols*.

Expertly designed, researched, and Holy Spirit inspired to provide you an extensive wealth of revelation knowledge about symbols and symbolic actions, this book is divided into four parts that go way beyond listing and defining words. Rhema word and divine prompting lift off every page!

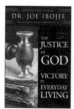

The Justice of God: Victory in Everyday Living—NEW

Only once in awhile does a book bring rare insight and godly illumination to a globally crucial subject. This book is one of them! A seminal work from a true practitioner, best-selling author, and leader of a vibrant church, Dr. Joe Ibojie brings clarity and a hands-on perspective to the Justice of God.

The Justice of God reveals:

- How to pull down your blessings.
- How to regain your inheritance.
- The heavenly courts of God.
- How to work with angels.
- The power and dangers of prophetic acts and drama.

The Watchman: The Ministry of the Seer in the Local Church—NEW

The ministry of the watchman in a local church is possibly one of the most common and yet one of the most misunderstood ministries in the Body of Christ. Over time, the majority of these gifted people have been driven into reclusive lives because of relational issues and confusion surrounding their very vital ministry in the local church.

Through the pages of *The Watchman* you will learn:

- Who these watchmen are.
- How they can be recognized, trained, appreciated, and integrated into the Body of Christ.
- About their potential and how they can be channelled as valuable resources to the local leadership.
- How to avoid prophetic and pastoral pitfalls.
- How to receive these gifted folks as the oracles of God they really are.

The 21st century watchman ministry needs a broader and clearer definition. It is time that the conservative, narrow, and restrictive perspectives of the watchman's ministry be enlarged into the reality of its great potential and value God has intended.

Korean translations:
Dreams and Visions volume 1

Italian translation:
Dreams and Visions Volume 1